MW00759743

IN THE NAME OF

LIBERTY

—— AND ——

DEMOCRACY

PERSONAL REFLECTIONS ON CIVIL RIGHTS
AND THE WAR IN VIETNAM

R. LEE MAHEE

Evelyn –
Please Enjoy the Book
R. Lee Mahee
10/12/2024

In The Name of Liberty and Democracy

Copyright © 2024 by R. Lee Mahee

ISBN: 978-1639457878(hc)
ISBN: 978-1639457861(sc)
ISBN: 978-1639457885(e)

Library of Congress Control Number: 2024913468

Writers' Branding
(877) 608-6550
www.writersbranding.com
media@writersbranding.com

CONTENTS

PREFACE

I began thinking about writing this manuscript after returning from Hanoi in 2011 where I taught an MBA class on leadership. My trip to Hanoi provided an opportunity for me, a college professor, to meet the citizens of Hanoi, many of whom were the sons and daughters, and even grandchildren, of my former enemy. I was a soldier during the war in Vietnam ('Nam). I found writing to be very therapeutic as I wrestled with my wartime memories. The more I wrote, the more I came to realize that for me, and for many Americans during the Vietnam era, we were in a two-front war. We were fighting in Vietnam, ostensibly to stop the spread of communism, while at home the fight was on to advance civil rights. In this book, I give personal reflections on the fight for civil rights and the war in Vietnam. The stories in this book are based upon my recollection, and much of the dialogue has been re-created from memory. In some instances, names and identifying characteristics of people and locations were changed to protect the privacy of those depicted.

Over the period covered by this writing, black people were referred to by various names. In the late 1950s and 60s, a black person was commonly referred to as colored or Negro. By the mid-1960s the preferred name became black, with a lowercase "b", as in an adjective referring simply to one's color. And though the term African-American was used as early as in the 1700s

(Schuessler, 2015), it was not commonly used as an identifier to describe a black person until the 1980s.

The MacArthur Foundation, whose mission is to "support creative people and effective institutions committed to building a more just, verdant, and peaceful world," noted on their website that The Foundation made a decision to update their writing style guide to treat race as a noun rather than as an adjective (Mack & Palfrey, 2020). The Foundation contends that race is more than a descriptor, "It is an indicator of personhood, culture, and history." Therefore, when referring to race in this manuscript, I have chosen to capitalize both Black and White.

I have also chosen to capitalize the word veteran when referring to a veteran of a specific war, for example, Korean War Veteran, World War II Veteran, Vietnam Veteran, in recognition of his or her service. This is consistent with the Veterans Affairs Style Guide.

Early in our marriage Jacqueline and I adopted the mantra, "supportive companions." I would like to dedicate this book to my wife Jacqueline and acknowledge her for inspiring me to write it. Every step along the way, Jackie helped me address the many intrusive and unwanted thoughts that would creep into my head, and she helped me to deal with my many emotionally troubling memories. She helped by having me focus on the positive people who have been and are in my life, and the many constructive activities in which I participated, a number of which I write about herein.

INTRODUCTION

In 1958, a group of New York City Boy Scouts traveled by chartered bus to the Philmont Scout Ranch in northern New Mexico, near the town of Cimarron. Two of the Scouts were Black: my best friend, Robert, and me. The group stayed at Air Force bases and an Indian reservation; and though it was a truly rich and extraordinary experience for all of us, many years later I came to suspect that the reason we stayed at those federally recognized facilities—as interesting as they were for young Scouts—was because of Jim Crow. You see, in the South back then, Robert and I being Black, "Negroes," we would not have been welcomed at "white-only" establishments. And though I cannot recall ever explicitly learning about segregation in school, as the years went by, I learned more and more about the Jim Crow laws and racial segregation from my readings, personal experiences, and cultural osmosis. I read about how poorly Blacks were treated in the South, and of the heinous assaults on Blacks that took place south of the Mason-Dixon. I began to notice how Blacks were even disregarded at home in the North. Now, as I look in the rearview mirror some sixty years later, I realize that Jim Crow, and racism generally, was closer to me personally than I had realized growing up in Harlem.

In 1959, John Howard Griffin, a White man, darkened his skin in an attempt to understand life as a Black in the Southern states. It wasn't until probably five years after Philmont (I would have been sixteen years old) when I got around to reading his 1961 work, *Black Like Me*, in which he recounted his travels into the Deep South, disguised as a Negro (Griffin 1962). Reading the book was emotionally draining, and it not only brought into clear view my travels into the Deep South with the Boy Scouts, but it also reminded me of the time my mother sent my brother Ralph (aka Ralphy or little Ralph) and me to "vacation" with her friends in Virginia for the summer, circa 1954. I was about seven or eight years old then and had not yet come to fully appreciate how different Black life was in the South from the live Blacks led in New York City. I vaguely recalled having to move to the back of the train in Washington, DC, as it prepared to head to Southern cities. And as I recall the train gradually pulling from the station, it slowly brought into focus my parents' final instructions. They insisted that I listen to, and follow without question, the directives given to me by all of the people living in Virginia, both Black and White … even kids my age.

Listening to Southern Blacks was important because they understood the rules of the game; listening to Southern Whites was important because they were the rule-makers. My mother knew, for my well-being, that I would have to succumb to the Southern Black way of life, and that she herself could not detail all of the do's and don'ts to which I must adhere. Of course, I didn't listen. I was from New York City. Harlem! When told not to go around the side of the house in Virginia where we stayed, I became inquisitive and just had to find out why they were prohibiting me. Stinging insects—yellow jackets or bees— attacked me. I was treated with a home remedy, recovered, and most importantly, I learned that day, that very day, that I must listen to those who knew the local milieu best. It would be a lesson on the importance of context, that is, I must learn from those who know the environment and situation and not assume that I can wallow my way through.

So why did my mother send me to Virginia in the first place, since she knew that by doing so, she would be putting me in harm's way? She was an avid reader, and she especially enjoyed reading about successful women; and there have been a number of successful Black women in Virginia. Women like Maggie Lena Walker. Maggie was born in Richmond about the time the Civil War was coming to an end. She became involved with an organization dedicated to the social and financial advancement of Blacks, started a department store, and established a bank that was able to survive the Great Depression (Norwood). Perhaps my mother had read about Irene Morgan, who brought suit in 1946 to desegregate interstate bus travel (Author: U.S. Supreme Court of Appeals, 2020). Her suit predated the Freedom Riders (History.com Editors, 2010a) and it was before Rosa Parks' 1955 refusal to relinquish her seat in the "colored section" of a Montgomery, Alabama, city bus to a White passenger (History.com Editors, 2009). Mother may have sent us to Virginia because, as it is noted on the website of the Virginia Museum of History & Culture:

> Although African Americans were confined to the lowest-paying industrial jobs, the need to provide services to other African Americans led to the emergence of a black middle class that included physicians, lawyers, funeral parlor directors, teachers, and ministers. Although the Renaissance may have been centered in Harlem in New York City, the growth of black cultural life emerged in urban communities throughout Virginia as well ("Jim Crow to Civil Rights in Virginia | Virginia Museum of History & Culture").

Ms. Nita, as she was called by the people in the neighborhood (or just Nita, by the family and close friends), was not formally educated. She left school before reaching the ninth grade, but contrary to what that might suggest, she was quite ambitious and persistent and had an innate understanding of business.

About the same time I "vacationed" in Virginia, Emmett Till, at age fourteen, was visiting Money, Mississippi, which, back then, had a population of approximately four hundred people. Like me, Emmett was from a Northern urban city. He was from Chicago. Money was no Chicago, and Mississippi was no Virginia. According to statistics from the archives at Tuskegee Institute, 539 Blacks were lynched in Mississippi from 1882 through 1968 (approximately six per year) while only 83 Blacks (less than one per year) were lynched in Virginia those years. Like my mother had done for me, Emmett's mother instructed him as to how he must conduct himself in the South. And like me, he did not heed his mother's instructions for he, like me, did not fully grasp what it meant to be Black in the South.

Inappropriately, it was claimed, poor Emmett Till flirted with a White woman in a store, a huge Black/White social taboo from which he would not recover. You see, back then, chiefly in the South, many White men considered White women as "cherished property." Black men, even boys the age of Emmett, were seen as "sex-crazed" and not properly socialized; in other words, threats to society. Three nights after allegedly offending a White woman (Tyson 2017), Emmett was beaten, shot, his eyes were gouged out, and he was dumped into the Tallahatchie River.

Then there was Willie Edwards, a truck driver, who members of the Ku Klux Klan believed was dating a White woman. In January 1957, a year before I was traveling to Philmont, Willie was forced to jump into the Alabama River, according to a signed affidavit from one of the accused murderers. His body was found months later. Alabama officials investigating the case said that his body was so decomposed that they could not declare his death a homicide. Nearly twenty years later, the state attorney general reopened the case, and even then, the judge said, "Being forced off a bridge is not necessarily a cause for death" (Tyson 2017).

When faced with racism back then, Northern Blacks, I would argue from mostly personal experience and reflection, felt a sense of righteous indignation, while Southern Blacks, it seems to me, realized clearly that there was a line—a bloody, red line—which, if crossed, would be to put one's life on the line. I could only imagine what it might have felt like to walk the streets of the South with a fear of being lynched because of my skin color. I was not afraid to vacation in Virginia because my mother had not warned me directly, because she wanted me to enjoy myself. But I was told to "listen to those who knew the local milieu best," which allowed me to maintain a sense of self-worth while at the same time learning early an important lesson that would be reinforced many years later in the Army.

Griffin's book was only the first of a series of stories I came across where a person of one race assumed the persona of someone of another race. Unlike Griffin, whose purpose was to experience Southern Black life, racial impostures I believe deceive others as to their true identity for one of a number of reasons, including: low self-esteem, personal gain, and/or to simply fit in with a particular demographic group.

In the Harlem community back in the day, light-skinned Blacks were admired, especially tall, light-skinned men. They were thought to be, and treated as if they were, the upper crust of the Black community. Contrary to what many believe, a young Black man—who looked White—by the name of Harry Murphy was actually the first Black student admitted (circa 1945) to the University of Mississippi (Ole Miss), and not James Meredith (Apel 2014). However, Meredith was not only Black; he looked Black, and so he is credited for being the first Black Ole Miss student.

Regardless of skin complexion, under the "one drop" rule, a person with even a negligible amount of Black blood from his or her ancestry is considered Black. Even so, in my Harlem community, it was known that lighter-skinned Blacks were generally treated by society with more respect than darker-skinned Blacks, and they were frequently able to obtain positions and profit professionally and financially because of their lighter skin tones (Cervantes-Anguas, 2021). Some Blacks, particularly women, would go as far as to use Nadinola, a bleaching skin cream, to lighten their complexion. As one Nadinola ad claimed, "The nicest things happen to girls with light, bright complexions!" (Kendi 2017)

Actress Carol Channing, who played in Hello, Dolly!, knew as early as 1937 that she was not White. Her biological father was a 'colored' man. As she was preparing for college her mother told her that her father was actually a Black man from Augusta, Georgia, and not (as she had come to believe) a White journalist from Rhode Island. Her mother wanted her to know this truth before possibly being surprised someday, should she have a Black baby (Channing 2002).

Harlem's Congressman Adam Clayton Powell, Jr. was of African American, Native American, and German ancestry (BlackPast 2008). His high school transcripts, which accompanied his Colgate application indicated that he was White (Jeffrey & Sportelli), and for a while he used his White-like appearance to his advantage at the University (Wikipedia 2019). In the spring of his freshman year, following a lecture given on campus by his father Adam Clayton Powell, Sr. many concluded that Adam Clayton, Powell, Jr. was Black.

"I can't live with you anymore because of the way your father defended Negroes today — you must be a Negro!" (Powell 2002, 35) insisted his roommate and friend… former friend.

More recently, presidential candidate Elizabeth Warren acknowledged being a Native American, probably of the Cherokee Nation, earning her the nickname "Pocahontas" by President

Donald Trump. A DNA test supervised by a respected geneticist supported Warren's assertion that she has Native American heritage, just as DNA has shown that Richard B. Spencer, the American neo-Nazi and White supremacist, is actually a Black man ... that is, according to the "one drop" rule. He is 99.5 percent European, but the remaining 0.5 percent is mostly African with a small trace of East Asian and Native American factored in (Flanagan 2018).

It has been said that "being Black" in America is to have a life sentence without the possibility of parole, for no amount of good behavior will change the amount of eumelanin in Black skin to set Blacks free. Griffin's pseudo-Black experience was not for the full sentence because he was paroled ... that is, he let himself become White again, setting himself free. However, being Black is more than a matter of skin color. It is about how we understand ourselves and how others understand us. Being Black in American can constrain one's thinking and bind one's heart and spirit. During the civil rights era, Blacks lived like birds in a gilded cage, and some of us would even be told by seemingly sympathetic non-Blacks, "You are different; not like the others."

What was Griffin looking to gain from a Black experience? Was empathy a driving force for him? Perhaps Griffin's motivation for changing his identity was starkly different than that of most racial imposters in that he may have truly wanted to temporarily give up his White privilege in 1959 to experience the life of a Black man. What a gutsy move! He was, in my estimation, attempting to advance in his field of study, which was ethnology.

Griffin was educated in the French language, literature, and medicine, and I believe he was genuinely interested in understanding the impact that the unhealthy relationship between Blacks and Whites, which existed since the days of slavery, has on society. Supporting my thinking is that, while serving as a medic for the French Resistance, he helped Austrian Jews escape to freedom in England. As a member of the United States Army Air Corps, he was assigned to study the culture of the Solomon Islands, where he was stationed for two years and first became interested in ethnology (Griffin 2019). It seems clear to me that Howard Griffin's background and his passion for ethnology account for why he would want to impersonate a Black person.

My belief as to Howard Griffin's motives for imitating a Black man were reinforced when I learned about Rachel Dolezal (Karimi 2018), another White person, this time a woman, who presented herself as Black and became president of the Spokane, Washington, NAACP for about a year, ending in 2015. Also, she served as Chair of the Office of Police Ombudsman Commission. Then her true identity was publicly made known. The media firestorm that rocked Dolezal's life, according to CNN, stemmed from family strife, and it was her own relatives who revealed that she was actually born White (Karimi 2018).

As I reflected on the civil rights movement of the 1950s and '60s, it was as if I was observing my life through a side-view mirror where my memories appeared a lot closer now—and more vivid—than they had actually appeared at any time in the past, less so when they had occurred.

As I reminisced about the 1950s, I recalled having to do air-raid drills because "the Russians were coming." In the '50s, the Russians were testing their nuclear bombs, and we were all afraid that they would someday drop a bomb on the US, as we had done on Japan's cities of Hiroshima and Nagasaki in 1945. In school, we were taught to line up against the wall or to crawl under our desks, which were fastened to the floor. We were taught to "duck and cover." At home, when the siren sounded, one could run into the vestibule of an apartment building, and even my apartment building was designated as an air-raid shelter. When in the apartment, we would stay away from the window and climb under the bed. I recall peeking out of the window one time and having Aunt Margaret scream at me to get inside and find cover. Margaret wasn't really my aunt but my friend Robert's aunt, and she volunteered to be a civil defense (CD) warden. She looked official with her CD armband and helmet as she watched for enemy planes and for civilians like me who did not heed the standing instructions of the Federal Civil Defense Administration. I would stand by the window and watch Aunt Margaret, not to challenge her authority, but in awe of her importance to the defense of our nation against Communist aggression. And because she was a strong and courageous woman, like the person my mother projected. I was proud to know her.

I remembered how, in the '50s and '60s, Black veterans of World War II would strut proudly as victors on the US team (albeit a segregated one) that defeated the Germans, the Japanese, and the Italian Fascists. For Black Soldiers, it was a two-front war for democracy and liberty; a fight for President Roosevelt's "Four Freedoms for all: freedom of speech, freedom of worship, freedom from want and freedom from fear" (Roosevelt). Roosevelt's 1941 Executive Order 8802 advanced this cause by giving job opportunities in the defense industry during the war to civilian workers, men and women, both Black and White.

However, it was not until I was drafted into the Army, sent to Vietnam, and returned home that I came to realize that my view of the American society was perhaps greatly distorted. Even as a Black man! I was to learn that Blacks fought in every American war, including the American Revolution and in 'Nam, hoping that their sacrifices would be acknowledged, and hoping that, as a result, they would earn the respect and get the benefits of a full US citizen. Put succinctly by Frederick Douglass:

Once let the black man get upon his person the brass letters, U.S.; let him get an eagle on his button, and a musket on his shoulder and bullets in his pocket, and there is no power on earth which can deny that he has earned the right to citizenship (*Military service 2013*).

Not happening! Full citizenship, that is. Hundred of thousands of Blacks fought in World War I and World War II, expecting to return stateside to welcoming arms only to be mistreated, to have their homes torched, and some men were even lynched.

VIETNAM, A RETURN

The total travel time from Philadelphia International Airport to our final destination, with layovers, was going to be, according to the itinerary, twenty-four hours and twenty minutes. After traveling a little more than nineteen hours, we landed at the Hong Kong International Airport, where we were to have some terra-firma time. We sat near the gate, patiently waiting to board the flight to Hanoi. Sitting behind my wife and me were a group of teenagers, probably Vietnamese, seemingly waiting for the same flight. They were playing cards. I don't know for certain, but I suspect they were playing Tiến Lên, a popular Vietnamese card game introduced at home by Vietnam Vets as a game called Vietcong or VC. As I watched the youngsters play, I thought about how they might be the children (or, even more likely, the grandchildren) of the men and women who had supported Ho Chi Minh's vision for a unified and independent Vietnam… then our enemy. It was an emotional moment as I reflected on my "in-country" experience forty years prior.

Sitting across from me was a distinguished-looking gentleman reading a book, a Westerner I gathered, perhaps from the States or the UK or maybe even Australia? He, too, was obviously on his way to Hanoi. I wondered what was taking him into the Communist country.

I turned to my wife, Jackie, and whispered, "What business do you think that gentleman across from us is in?"

She thought for a moment as she glanced at him, and then replied, "He may be in retail clothing, a buyer, perhaps ... it is anyone's guess."

However, her guess was not surprising because when we shopped for lightweight clothing to wear in Hanoi's hot and humid July weather, we found many of the items we bought were actually made in Vietnam. Vietnam, having won the "American War," was now a unified and independent Communist country that was doing business with the United States. The gentleman must have felt our eyes on him, for he suddenly looked up and caught us gazing at him. To avoid appearing rude, I spoke. "Hi, I gather you, too, are going to Hanoi."

"Yes," he responded, introducing himself as Arthur and asking, "what takes you to Hanoi?"

"I will be teaching an accelerated MBA course to North Vietnamese students. A course in leadership," I said, as I laughed to myself, *and they won the war.* My response indicated that I had not yet come to grips with the fact that there was no longer a South Vietnam, nor a North Vietnam, but just a Vietnam.

I was a full-time faculty member of a historically black university (HBCU), which was offering classes in Hanoi to students from various countries ... even Communist countries like Russia and China. Full-time faculty members were often asked to teach a summer course. Some professors wanted to teach in the summer as a way of earning additional income, others (for whom home was in India or Africa) would go to Vietnam to teach and from there would travel home, thereby greatly reducing their travel expense. I didn't like teaching summers because, by the time I entered academe, I was in my fourth career, and I was both emotionally and financially ready for retirement. However, when asked to teach for three weeks in Vietnam for the MBA Program, I was intrigued and ecstatic, and so I agreed.

I continued the conversation with Arthur, saying, "I will be in Hanoi for a few weeks ... actually, nineteen days, and I hope to see a great deal of Hanoi while I'm there. I'm Richard, by the way," introducing myself, and saying, "this is my wife, Jackie."

After greeting Jackie, Arthur asked more specifically about what I was going to teach, about the program I was going to teach under, and all the time showing great interest in my endeavor. His questions unearthed in me the realization that I was on my way to Hanoi, not to face the fearsome enemy I had once known, but to teach the sons and daughters of that enemy. And though intellectually I had accepted that Vietnam was no longer divided into north and south, emotionally for me, and perhaps for most other former GIs of the Vietnam War,there would always be a North Vietnam and a South Vietnam, for our suffering and our personal wartime experiences and the way we were treated upon returning home, albeit decades ago, would not let us see it any other way. Saigon, now Ho Chi Minh City, will always exist in the hearts and minds of many of us as Saigon.

"What about you, Arthur?" I asked.

"I am a consultant working for the US government. I'm here to help the Vietnamese work on the health of their banking system."

With a slight grin, I looked for confirmation of what I'd heard. "The US is sending consultants to help the Vietnamese banking system?" *Was he kidding? Doesn't the Vietnamese government follow US news? Are they not aware that the US government spent billions of dollars bailing out US banks?* So, I asked, "Is the Vietnamese government looking to bail out its banks?"

"Not exactly," Arthur commented. "The Vietnamese are particularly interested in learning how to stress-test their financial institutions, which is something I am not an expert in, but they keep insisting that I help them, and so I will."

"Ah," I remarked, as I began to ponder why Arthur would be interested in the assignment since he acknowledged to me at least that he was not adept at bank stress-testing. For Arthur, I concluded, it was an opportunity to broaden his offerings as a consultant... Americans, I would argue—and now Vietnamese, perhaps—will play the hand they have to win. They may have a winning hand or may have to bluff. Arthur was going to bluff his way through.

As Arthur and I talked, I noticed people were beginning to gather around the airline counter and were preparing to board the flight. Arthur reached for his bag. If there had been a boarding announcement, it escaped me. Jackie apparently had missed it, too, because she did not make a move to ready herself for boarding until I stood.

Could we have missed the call for the flight because it was not in English? Then I thought, *why would I expect to hear announcements in English?* Perhaps I needed a mindset calibration. In haste, I proceeded to the restroom, concerned that I might miss my flight. On my way, I did not hesitate to say chào to people whom I passed along the way, a term I remembered from my Vietnam War days to mean hello. I hoped I was not offending anyone by attempting to speak in Vietnamese; after all, I was in China. Was my attempt to be kind and courteous by speaking Vietnamese while in China actually rude? Should I have addressed everyone in English?

At 10:40 p.m., we boarded Trans North Aviation Flight 518 for Hanoi, Vietnam, and as we boarded, Arthur handed me a business card with his Hanoi address and telephone number. "Give me a call," he suggested, "and perhaps we can have dinner some evening," noting that he knew a number of really fine restaurants in Hanoi. Apparently, Arthur had been to Hanoi on several occasions, and he knew his way around. Having someone like Arthur willing to introduce us to the city was a real blessing and we looked forward to taking him up on his offer. The two-hour flight was scheduled to arrive at 11:40 p.m. local time. As the plane took to the air, a strong emotion came over me from the realization that I was once again in Southeast Asia. I glanced out of the window and reflected on my high school days, and what brought me to Vietnam the first time. The first time as a soldier in the fight against Communism.

Gazing out of the window of the plane, I could see the lights of Hanoi shining brightly, lighting the sky, as did illumination rounds shot by the North Vietnamese from Russian-made antiaircraft guns during American B-52 bombings of Hanoi. And as the plane began its descent, I thought about what men such as Captain John McCain (later Senator John McCain) and other US Naval and Air Force aviators might have seen as they flew over the city. Suddenly, the plane hit air pockets; it was as though the plane was under attack, or so I could imagine, giving me a vague sense as to what it must have been like being a member of a bomber flight crew over Hanoi; Senator John McCain was shot down over Hanoi during such a bombing mission. When I heard the loud noise and felt the vibrations from the landing gears dropping, I regained my composure. We landed at the Hanoi Noi Bai International Airport at about 11:30 p.m. Indochina Time (ICT) and promptly began to disembark. Within minutes, I touched the ground of Hanoi, North Vietnam, not as a soldier, but as a professor.

Surprisingly, deplaning in the Communist country of Vietnam was not much different from getting off a flight at any non-Communist international airport. It seemed that Noi Bai was just another international airport, at least for Jackie, who appeared quite excited to be in Hanoi. Her previous international travel was to Aruba, Bermuda, and Cancun, and so, for her to be able to travel outside of the western hemisphere was quite exhilarating. I enjoyed traveling as much as Jackie did, and in addition to going to Aruba, Bermuda, and Cancun, I had even worked a short time in London and Japan. And unlike Jackie, traveling to the eastern hemisphere was not as exciting because my job had sent me to Tokyo, and I had spent nineteen months in Pleiku, South Vietnam, at the US government's invitation. Consequently, I saw things differently than did Jackie, and unlike her, I was very apprehensive about being in Hanoi. My thoughts then turned to the year and a half I'd spent mostly with the 20th Combat Engineers in Pleiku. I thought especially about my last thirty days in 'Nam, which was after my battalion was pulled out in 1971, except for a small contingent of us who were left behind and attached to an ARVN (Army of the Republic of Vietnam) unit to support and advise them.

Though more than forty years had passed, my recollections of that time were like a tight shot group concentrated around my wartime experiences.

I was full of angst as we progressed through the airport. I could not help but notice that airport security was dressed in military-like uniforms and stood erect with a posture and poise that one would expect of Soldiers of the formidable enemy, as was the North Vietnamese Army. I found myself trying to inconspicuously pass by airport security as if to evade them. Suddenly, I realized that Jackie had gotten in line to process into the country while I was still wandering and looking around, as a lost or indecisive person might. I was behaving like one of those tourists I would see visiting Harlem, displaying great vigilance and circumspection. Surely, my cautious, guarded behavior did not go unnoticed. I hurriedly joined Jackie in line and began processing in. We processed through visa and passport control without a hitch, then we got our bags from baggage claim and proceeded through customs without a problem.

After processing into Hanoi, pulling our suitcases behind us, Jackie and I were off to meet Michael, the American who worked in Hanoi for the university's MBA Program. I did not really know Michael, but I had the opportunity to communicate with him via email several times before coming to Hanoi and I'd learned that our lives had intersected. He was a New Yorker, as was I. We had both attended high schools in the Bronx. I went to DeWitt Clinton, and he attended Evander Childs High School just a short distance, walking distance, away from DeWitt. I looked forward to meeting Michael and felt somewhat assured that Jackie and I would be in good hands with him. Even so, reminiscing about 'Nam, thinking about the war protestors who welcomed me home, and wondering how the citizens of Hanoi might see me, all contributed to making me feel less than comfortable about being in Hanoi with only Michael as my guide.

Soon we were headed for the ground transportation area where we were to be met by Michael. And as we walked down the corridor, I looked timorously into the eyes of the Vietnamese men and women and wondered what they might be thinking … were they pondering, as we had about Arthur, as to what brought us to Hanoi?

I was also apprehensive because, supposedly, a disproportionately large number of Blacks had served in combat units during the war, and we had done more than our fair share of inflicting pain and heartache on the North Vietnamese people on behalf of the American government. Had I been an American World War II Veteran visiting Berlin years after that war, I might have felt somewhat anxious but would have walked the streets of Berlin with pride, for I would have been ecstatic that I'd contributed to winning the war against the racist Adolph Hitler. I could only imagine what the person passing by me in the Hanoi airport might have been thinking. To give me emotional strength, I hypothesized that they saw me as a veteran coming to pay homage to the city on which the US had brought great devastation.

As I walked down the corridor, I kept in mind that the North Vietnamese were sophisticated people, sophisticated enough to know that the American Army had been in great part conscripted, and that many Blacks had been drafted because we were mostly poor and politically powerless, and consequently, could not escape the draft. They knew that, mostly against our will, we had to serve two years in the military with one of the two years in Vietnam, which could be a death sentence, particularly for draftees who received as little as sixteen weeks of training before being sent into combat.

> Approximately 300,000 African Americans served in the Vietnam War. In 1965, African Americans filled 31% of the ground combat battalions in Vietnam, while the percentage of African Americans as a minority in the general population was 12%. In 1965, African Americans suffered 24% of the U.S. Army's fatal casualties (*American minority groups in the Vietnam War: A resource guide: Introduction*).

I suspected that they also knew that American willpower would flounder because the folks in the States had a front-row seat to the daily televised showings of the "horrors of war." American media reported daily to our family and friends the number of US lives lost as it rose into the tens of thousands, even as they informed us that enemy forces lost climbed into the hundreds of thousands of people.

Now a college professor, I was to come face-to-face amicably with the "Charles" family, some of whom were now adult college students and whom, even as youngsters, may have fought against the US. More likely, they were students who had lost a parent, grandparent, or other relative in the conflict. I was "in-country" then, as a US GI fighting against Communism, and now I've returned, albeit apprehensively, to serve in Hanoi as a professor educating Communist students, helping them gain their MBA degrees from an American university … an HBCU. I pondered the relationship between the various factions, the US: its government, its people (all of its people), and the historically black university; Vietnam: the people of what was formerly South Vietnam, and the people of formerly North Vietnam, now the victorious unified Socialist Republic of Vietnam. I wondered how these factions, and the relationships among them, had changed over the forty years since I was first in-country, more importantly, since we lost the war.

It was well after midnight. Wandering down the corridor of the Noi Bai airport at night in search of the ground transportation area reminded me of the trepidation I'd felt as a commander of relief roving along the bunker line at Engineer Hill in Pleiku, and reminiscing about Pleiku made me very uncomfortable as I reflected on my former Vietnam life. We continued to head toward the ground transportation area where we were to be met by Michael.

Michael was to take Jackie and me to our hotel, an important thing since we had no clue how to get around in Hanoi, and we did not speak Vietnamese. More importantly, we had no idea which hotel the University had booked for us. Michael was waiting in the ground transportation area as planned, with a large sign bearing our name so that we could easily identify him. We could not have missed him. He was the only White fellow waiting in the pickup area, and he looked much like I had imagined he would from my brief conversations with him before we'd left the States. He was young, blonde, and of medium build. He appeared to be in his early forties, some twenty years younger than Jackie and I.

After we greeted one another, he took us to where the taxis were lined up waiting to carry arrivals to their destination. We got into line and waited patiently for our chance to get one. When it was our turn, we climbed into a Mai Linh cab, and

Michael surprised me by speaking in English, not Vietnamese. He told the driver where we wanted to go, naming the Sunway Hotel. Before he spoke, I'd assumed that Michael would speak in Vietnamese, but the cab driver understood English. I found that consoling. Also, I recalled that some airport signs were in English, and I learned during our cab trip that Michael spoke very little Vietnamese. That meant Jackie and I would be able to get around in Hanoi with little difficulty.

Subsequently, I learned that Michael had little interest in learning the Vietnamese language, or even about its culture. I did not ask him directly about his lack of interest because I thought such a question would be inappropriate, at least until I got to know him a bit better. I would expect that most expats would want to learn the official language of the country. No longer was I apprehensive about being in Hanoi. I could get around in English. *But what brought Michael to Vietnam?*

"So, tell me about the Sunway Hotel," I said. He replied by saying that the hotel was just walking distance to the school. He saw this as a positive; I saw it as a concern. I was to teach in the evening from 6:00 to 10:00 p.m. I had not gone into the city of Pleiku in the evening during the war; I was not fond of walking around my Harlem neighborhood at night; and I am expected to walk the streets of Hanoi at six and ten every night. Concerning! The idea that I would have to walk back and forth, the same time each evening, to school worried me. If there was one lesson that I'd learned from my Vietnam War experience it was this: "It is dangerous to make it a habit to travel the same path on the same schedule."

THE SUNWAY

I continued to ponder what had brought Michael to Vietnam in the first place and why he was continuing to live here. Without me having to ask, Michael explained during our thirty-minute cab trip from the Noi Bai airport to 19 Pham Dinh Ho Street, the Sunway Hotel, that he was greatly disappointed in the United States government. He expressed strong feelings against the US because of the many wars and conflicts it had gotten into ... under the pretense of furthering liberty and democracy around the world. He rattled off a few of those conflicts while saying, "The US tries to push its form of democracy onto others. The US invaded Grenada and Panama, and took it upon itself to reinstate Aristide in Haiti." I was a soldier in one of those wars, the Vietnam War, which he did not mention, maybe because he didn't want a personal conflict with me.

I think Jackie was as taken aback as I by his comments. He paused from speaking and began gazing out of the cab window. During those few moments, no one spoke. Then Michael, who seemed to be deep in thought about what he had said, began glancing back and forth between the window and me. "There was also Kosovo, Iraq, and Afghanistan," he said in a whisper. Raising his voice just a few decibels, he continued, "You know, many of America's own people are still being treated unfairly..." This was a statement I fully understood and shared, but his use of the phrase "America's own people" made me wonder if he was distancing himself … I wondered if he continued to think of himself a United States citizen. Was Michael a Communist? As I thought about what Michael alleged, I remembered reading about the 1950s and the Korean War. I'd turned eight in 1955 and had only a fuzzy recollection of that time, but I'd read about it. I had personally encountered the effects of McCarthyism, having been reared (I was not permitted to use "raised" in grade school when referring to a human) in Harlem. Perhaps he was Communist.

Ultimately, the important question for me was not if he was a Communist, but why was Michael in Hanoi? How had he ended up in Hanoi? He was too young to have fought in the Vietnam War, and he was obviously against—strongly against—the US spreading its political ideology throughout the world. And though he had not said so, Michael was, at least from the impression I was getting, a Communist and a student of history. It all made sense. He was working for an HBCU and was sympathetic to the struggles of Blacks in our fight for civil rights, as was the Communist Party after the Great Depression (Kelley 1990, 57-78).

At last, we pulled in front of the Sunway Hotel in Hanoi's Hai Ba Trung district. Michael mentioned that professors from my HBCU who'd previously taught in Hanoi stayed at a hotel in the Hoan Kiem district (the Old Quarter), which is the business and tourist area. "The Sunway will be your home for the nineteen days you're here," Michael told me. I was convinced that the school had booked the hotel in the Hai Ba Trung district not for my purposes, but for theirs. The University wanted to reduce its hotel expense, and the school wanted our program to be in Hai Ba Trung because it's where many of Vietnam's best universities are located. In Hai Ba Trung, you can find the Hanoi University of Technology, the Hanoi National Economics University, the

Hanoi University of Civil Engineering, and the Hanoi University of Pharmacy ... And now the graduate business program of an HBCU. I found it curious that Hanoi and an HBCU would agree to offer graduate business courses. Ultimately, I reflected not on the fact that I would be located near the great universities of Vietnam, or that I was there to teach an MBA leadership course, but rather what the Hai Ba Trung district symbolized to the Vietnamese people, and to me as a Vietnam Veteran.

The Hai Ba Trung district was named after the Trung sisters who, with an army composed mostly of women, had led the first rebellion against an occupying Chinese Army in AD 40 but was ultimately defeated. The Trung sisters have always been revered throughout Vietnam as symbolizing Vietnam's independence (Gandhi 2022; History 101 2022). Historically, Vietnamese women not only fought alongside men in combat but also led men in battle. In the US, women were not allowed to join the combat arms until Secretary of Defense Leon Panetta removed the restriction on women serving in combat on January 24, 2013. Is it possible we learned about women in combat after watching Vietnamese women participate in the Vietnam War?

Michael, Jackie, and I entered the hotel lobby of the Sunway at about 12:45 a.m. (ICT) and proceeded directly to the front desk. We were exhausted after having traveled for more than twenty-four hours ... and boy, could we use a good night's rest! I approached the desk, and just before reaching it, I spoke out, a bit louder than my usual conversational voice, saying, "We have reservations arranged for us by my university." As I spoke, I glanced at the wall behind the manager and saw a sign, in Vietnamese and in English that read, "Visitors of guests are not allowed in hotel rooms. They must remain in the lobby." And before Michael could finish explaining that the sign was necessary because prostitution, though illegal in Hanoi, was rampant, the front-desk manager, without even checking his computer, let me know in broken English, "No reservation made for you at hotel." His English was certainly good enough for me to clearly get the message. We did not have a room. His statement sounded all too familiar. I could not help but wonder if I was being turned away because I was Black, or because the woman with me—my wife—was White and the manager could not perceive her as my legal partner. After all, the North Vietnamese had weaponized America's segregation during the war. While serving in 'Nam, the rumor was that the North Vietnamese and Vietcong gave preferential treatment to Black Soldiers they'd captured. They attempted to develop a "healthy" relationship with their Black captives because they understood our plight back home. Now the war was over, and they had won.

Michael intervened and told the manager he needed to make a phone call to clear things up. He asked Jackie and me to have a seat in the waiting area while he found out what was going on. I became increasingly edgy. I could not help but feel that racism was at play and that the manager, if not the hotel, did not want to provide us with a room. After nearly thirty minutes of deliberation, Michael was able to secure a room for us.

Before leaving the lobby, Michael gave us twenty-five million Vietnam dong (around one thousand dollars), a cell phone, and a list of important telephone numbers, including his personal cell number. He also gave us a taxicab card to be used for travel within Hanoi so that our travels would be charged directly to the University. On the card were the names of the cab services for which the card could be used. I recognized one of the cab companies, Mai Linh. After rendering all of these goodies, Michael bid us farewell, and the hotel bellhop, carrying our bags, escorted us to our room, which was on the third floor. He opened the door with a key card and inserted the card into a slot to turn on the lights. I had not seen a hotel that required the room's entry card to be used this way. My business acumen had me think, *What a wonderfully eco-friendly and money-saving idea!* It ensured that one would not leave the room with the lights on because the resident would need the card to regain entry into the room.

We both slept well our first night in Hanoi, though I awoke the next morning with a really bad cold and a headache. I guess sitting in a low-humidity airplane cabin in close proximity to other passengers for a long period of time makes one susceptible to catching whatever is generously being shared.

When she finally awoke Jackie's first question was, "How do you feel about being in Hanoi?" I knew she was really asking me how I felt, as a Vietnam War Veteran, about being in Hanoi. Unlike my colleagues at the University who would ask how I felt about going back to Vietnam, Jackie understood that I was not returning to the Vietnam I once knew.

The only Americans who made it to Hanoi during the war, as far as I know, were captured American servicemen like John McCain (who was a guests of the infamous Hanoi Hilton or other similar "resort" spots), journalists like Peter Arnett (who went with others to Hanoi to accept three American POWs), and Jane Fonda (who was the "distinguished" guest of the Democratic Republic of Vietnam, i.e., North Vietnam). For me, it was a trip behind enemy lines.

To dodge the intention of Jackie's question, I responded by saying, "I have a sore throat and feel extremely weak; I'm going to have to get plenty of bed rest this weekend so I'm ready to teach on Monday." It was Friday and my reply was my way of telling her that I planned to stay in bed all weekend. And also, certainly to her surprise, I gave no indication that I was in any way uneasy about being in Hanoi.

That weekend, the lyrics of "The Sound of Silence" by Simon & Garfunkel bounced around my head like a ball bouncing around the walls of a squash ball court.

I slept as well in Hanoi that weekend as I did most nights in Pleiku during the war. For now, I felt safe in the hotel room; it was my bunker. To further ease Jackie, I told her that my focus over the weekend was going to be on preparing to teach. It wasn't. It couldn't be. Though I had slept well most nights, my thoughts were always on 'Nam, the war. Thoughts about 'Nam remained with me day and night. I knew I would be in trouble if this trip to Hanoi turned out to be as traumatic as transitioning back into civilian life after 'Nam had been for me.

Immediately after we arose the first morning, Jackie began her routine of disinfecting the room, as she always does when we stay in a hotel. After the room was cleaned to her satisfaction, we began unpacking our suitcases and started putting away our clothes. It was then that Jackie concluded that the room was too small and that we would not be able to live comfortably for nearly three weeks in such cramped quarters. Probably not as cramped as John McCain's Hanoi digs were. So, before completely unpacking, Jackie called the front desk and requested a larger room. The hotel accommodated us. They sent up a bellboy to move us to our new room for which we would have to pay an additional nominal charge, at our (not the University's) expense. The room's price differential was fifty thousand dong. That was not a problem; we had twenty-five million dong. The increase in room charge turned out to be about two dollars—a small increase, as was the increase in room size. We went from teensy to tiny!

After settling into our new "spacious" room, we slept for many hours. We slept through the first day and night, getting up only for dinner. We thought about contacting Arthur to ask if we could join him for dinner, but it was getting late, and we had no idea how far his place was from the Sunway. Besides, it would be a little inconsiderate for us to suggest that we get together, given that Jackie seemed to be coming down with a cold or something, and I was—without question—ill. Instead, we decided to have dinner at the Sunway's Allante Restaurant, which was advertised as one of the best restaurants in Hanoi. It occupied an entire upper floor of the hotel and offered not only Vietnamese food, but international cuisine. It sounded really good.

As we stepped out of the elevator, the restaurant's host, without acknowledging my presence, asked Jackie how many we were. "Two," she responded. The host led us to a table and placed a menu at two places of the four-seat table. He walked around the table and pulled out a seat for Jackie, as one would expect the host to do at a first-class restaurant. I seated myself. He never acknowledged me. I ordered a steak dinner, while Jackie was more adventurous. I'm not sure exactly what she ordered, but it looked "un-American." Throughout the meal, our male server appeared to be uneasy with me (at least, I felt so), and when he left the check, he placed it on the table opposite Jackie, as if to suggest that she would be paying the tab. Was the treatment of me emblematic of the type of treatment that Jackie and I would sometimes experience as an interracial couple when dining back in the States, or was it an attitudinal remnant of 'Nam? Women did not serve in US combat arms, so clearly, she could not have been the enemy. I paid the bill with a smile and a tip of fifty thousand dong … two dollars. Subsequently, I learned that one was not expected to give any tip in Hanoi.

We remained in the room the remainder of the weekend, and ordered food to be brought to our room. I spent most of my time reading and fighting my cold, and I worked diligently to prepare for class. I had to work hard because leadership was not a course that I typically taught, but I'd accepted the assignment because I had wanted to visit Hanoi. Jackie, breaking her silence, laughingly whispered, "You are here to teach leadership and organizational behavior, and they won the war." She said it as though it was a revelation. Yes, I thought, we fought and lost the war that was to stop the Communist takeover of South Vietnam, and now here I was being sent to Communist Vietnam as a professor to teach a leadership course to the victors. Capitalism?

EVENING SCHOOL

In preparation to teach, I wondered why a student in Hanoi would take a leadership course from me, an American professor. One might conclude simply that some courses are required to get the degree. And for Vietnamese students, I imagined getting an MBA from an American university, any university in the States, would be prestigious and valuable. I presumed they realized that by entering an American MBA Program, they could change their life's trajectory. The students recognize, I believe, that they live in a global society, which means that the labor market is not just local (which could, for them, be limiting), but global. With an American graduate business degree in hand, they could possibly benefit from an American company's offshoring effort. There is an economic battle going on, and the Vietnamese students seemed to appreciate that education is a strategic weapon in that fight.

I continued to think about my course offering. I juxtapose my Hanoi students seeking an education through an American MBA Program and acquiring the technical skills needed to compete in business with being an American soldier completing Advanced Individual Training (AIT) mastering his craft and learning what it takes to survive. The Vietnamese students seemed most comfortable learning by rote, which was the way we were taught in AIT. Getting to the right answer was more important than understanding why or how you got there. Obviously, 'Nam still weighted heavily on my mind.

I thought about the possible differences between my HBCU students back home and the students in Hanoi who enrolled in the HBCU program. One big difference was that unlike my American HBCU students who typically could speak only one language, English, the Hanoi HBCU students, not only spoke Vietnamese, but could write and speak in English. And because Vietnam was once colonized by the French there were some who could speak French. Also, a few students could converse in Russian ... they chatted in Russian with my one Russian student. I guess I should not have been surprised since Russia was Hanoi's ally during the War.

> By several measures, the United States has neglected languages in its educational curricula, its international strategies, and its domestic policies. ... While English continues to be the lingua franca for world trade and diplomacy, there is an emerging consensus among leaders in business and politics, teachers, scientists, and community members that proficiency in English is not sufficient to meet the nation's needs in a shrinking world. (American Academy of Arts & Sciences 2022).

I recall, as a youngster, joking (though there was some serious concern) that we may all be speaking Russian someday if we lose the Cold War. In hindsight, the Cold War was an economic war, and we won. Then came the war with North Vietnam, and the domino theory. Winning the War, the Communists united North and South Vietnam under their rule. The domino theory is defunct now, and forty years after 'Nam, I am invited to teach an MBA course in English in Hanoi, though they won the war. Why? Economics I suppose. Vietnam is now open to foreign trade, business investments, educators like me, and students from other countries under their policy of economic democracy (Doi Moi).

In 2020, exports to Vietnam were $9.9 billion, and imports from Vietnam were $79.6 billion ("Vietnam" 2022). Let me emphasize: Vietnamese students with an American graduate business degree can benefit from doing business with the US, and they know it. For me, teaching students of Hanoi provided a wonderful opportunity to encounter the post-'Nam attitudes and perspectives of today's Vietnamese people in the north of the country toward Americans. I considered that Hanoi was just a segment of the Vietnamese population, and I wondered if the attitude I sensed was toward all Americans or just someone like me.

As I stepped toward the hotel room window, observing the people moving about in the street below, I wondered what I might do to make my classroom environment welcoming. I wondered to what extent I would be welcomed. I questioned whether I could use the General Colin Powell PowerPoint slide presentation on leadership that had been given to me by a fellow Rotarian just days before I'd left for Hanoi.

General Powell is one of my idols. Powell was born in Harlem, as was I; attended high school in the Bronx, as did I; and attended the City College of New York on 137th Street and Convent Avenue, which is on the other side of St. Nicholas Park from where I was reared. His PowerPoint presentation offers eighteen specific lessons on leadership. What General Powell offered was definitely applicable in a business setting. I hesitated to use the slides because on the slides, General Powell is dressed in a military uniform and I was not certain how the students would react. I was fairly certain, however, that they would recognize his name. I was also hesitant because all of my classes were to be videotaped, and I was not certain for what purpose or by whom. Was it the school or the Vietnamese government doing the taping? I was concerned that I would be putting myself in harm's way. Further, I didn't think it reasonable to teach a course on leadership in Hanoi, talk about the views of General Powell, and not recognize, and even discuss, the charismatic, powerful Vietnamese leader, Ho Chi Minh. Uncle Ho, as the Vietnamese commonly and affectionately referred to him as, was and remains the symbol of Vietnam's unification. After the Vietnam War, the city of Saigon was renamed Ho Chi Minh City. I had a lot of studying to do!

The next morning, Sunday, I decided to take a walk to the school to get a sense for how far it was from the hotel and how long it would take to get there. Though I was given a cab card and could ride there for free, I wanted to walk to be among the people, as frightening as it was. I took this trial walk on what was a very hot and humid day, and sweat poured from my every pore the very minute I stepped out of the hotel. I began my trek, walking slowly, very slowly, down Pham Dinh Ho Street toward Lò Đúc Street, all of the time cognizant of how wet my clothes were getting. I looked as though I had gotten caught in a sun-shower while no one else seemed to be perspiring. As I walked, I thought about having to fear two enemies in 'Nam: those outside of the barbwire, who were perhaps some of the same people I passed as I walked, and those within my own ranks in 'Nam, who greatly disliked me for who I was and what I stood for as a Black team leader.

I continued my walk down Lò Đúc Street toward the school, carrying my head up as to indicate that I belonged, and I walked with deliberation as if to suggest I knew exactly where I was going. I made certain my pace and posture were not like that of the White people I would see walking the streets of Harlem their first time. Also, in 'Nam, we were taught not to always walk the same path at the same time because that would give the enemy an opportunity to ambush us or to place a booby trap along the path to kill or maim us. Undoubtedly, the anxiety I felt from this thought added to my perspiration problem. But I was not a young man in Pleiku during the war, but in Hanoi many years afterward, and I felt certain that walking the same way to school Monday through Friday evenings and Saturday mornings would give the fine citizens of the city an opportunity to meet and greet me, not ambush me. My hope was that they would come to know me as a professor teaching their students, and for that reason would respect me, speak to me, and treat me as one of their own.

I awoke Monday morning ready to prepare to teach that evening. Shortly after getting up, I took one last pass over my class material to figure out how I might contrast the two leadership styles. To save time that day, I decided to eat breakfast and lunch at the Sunway's Allante Restaurant. I stayed in bed and rested much of the time so that I would not be too weak from the cold I'd had. I needed to be strong enough to teach that entire evening. The walk was going to take about ten minutes, and I wanted to get there early to meet my administrative help and the class leaders who were to help me with my classes. Michael promised to be there the first day to introduce me to my administrative assistant. Certainly, I wanted to get to class on time to give a good impression and to set the right tone from day one. I was all set to teach that evening and I knew the route to the school. Yet, I was uneasy, very uneasy, not about having to walk to school during dusk, but about having to walk back to the hotel from the school at ten at night.

I started my trek to the school at 5:30 that evening. On the corner of Pham Dinh Ho and Lò Đúc Streets was a young man sitting on his moped, which he had leaning on a pole. I said bravely, "Chào" (laughing to myself as I remembered using the greeting at the airport in China, but this time I expected to be understood). I was greatly relieved by his friendly facial expression and pleasant-sounding response, which of course, I did not understand. I just returned the smile. As I proceeded down Lò Đúc Street, I saw a number of people squatting or sitting on stools along the sidewalk. I also saw what appeared to be families sitting at tables in their storefront-like apartments, which I observed from the corner of my eye. Just a few feet from where I was walking, I could see people eating around a table or sitting on a sofa, and I could see people in back rooms lying in beds. A few of the men, and even some women, smiled and spoke as I walked by. The women who greeted me did so respectfully, unlike Pleiku's wartime boom-boom girls (prostitutes). Yet, there was no fooling me. To them, a Black man walking along Lò Đúc Street had to be a shocker! I wondered if they thought I was Montagnard (mountain people).

After the war, a number of human rights organizations have reported that the Socialist Republic of Vietnam had been killing off the Montagnard people in the Central Highlands, many of whom sided with America during the war. The possibility that they would confuse me for a Montagnard made me feel very much at risk.

In the midst of the Vietnam War, syndicated columnists Rowland Evans and Robert Novak described the advisory work the Green Berets were doing with Montagnards metaphorically:

> Assume that during our own Civil War the north had asked a friendly foreign power to mobilize, train, and arm hostile American Indian tribes and lead them into battle against the South ... The indigenous Montagnards, recruited into service by the American Special Forces in Vietnam's mountain highlands, defended villages against the Viet Cong and served as rapid response forces. The Special Forces and the Montagnards—each tough, versatile, and accustomed to living in wild condition ... (Onion 2022).

After the war, the Communist North executed some Montagnard leaders and sent others to prison or to a "reeducation" camp. Also, their cultural rights, education, and employment opportunities were limited (Southerland 2018) like they were for southern Blacks after American wars, and we were on the winning side of those war. Thus, the concern that I might be mistaken for a Yard (Montagnard) was completely justified and scary.

After walking the equivalent of two city blocks down Lò Đúc Street, I made a left and proceeded guardedly for 110 meters into the alley-like street that led to the school building. A couple of young men turned into the alley on motorbikes and followed behind me. I began to pick up the pace. The school building, which was now in sight, was at the very end of the alley another 50 meters away. I made every effort to get to the building before they could catch up with me. I even considered running, but that would signal that I was afraid, and I needed to maintain my composure … I needed to hold onto the little equanimity I had. Perspiration from the climatic heat and humidity was being augmented by sweat from nervousness. Pools of water began pouring from my brow. For certain, the motorbikes would overtake me before I reached the building. Would I be close enough to the building to be safe? If not, there was nothing, nothing, I would be able to do. They were on bikes, and I could not outrun them. They were several, and I was one. Then I noticed that more and more bikes, not all motorbikes, entered the alley. One after another, the bikes passed me as I stepped closer and closer to the wall to let them through. About five bikes, some with two people on them, passed me on my left as I walked, and not one person said anything to me. Within 25 meters of the large concrete school building, I noted that the young men whom I initially spotted following me parked their bikes, got off, and were carefully reaching into their bike pouches. I was beginning to feel extremely tense and my hands got sweaty. I started thinking about what I might do to protect myself if necessary, as I watched them gradually removing something from their pouches. It was copies of the books I'd ordered for class. Even though I was on my way to teach, I saw the young people around me, not possibly as students, but as adversaries. My head was still in 'Nam or back home in certain neighborhoods.

I entered the building and walked up the stairs to the second floor. I could have taken the elevator, but I was afraid. When I reached the second floor, students were standing around and having pre-class snacks provided by the university. The snacks were made available because most of the students were coming directly from work. I introduced myself, picked up what appeared to be a cup of tea, and joined them for a minute or two. It was the perfect opportunity for me to meet a few of the students in a more relaxed, social setting rather than in the more formal setting of the classroom. I then met with the assigned administrator and class leader. They gave me the class roster, and I gave them copies of my updated syllabus.

From talking with colleagues who had previously taught in Hanoi, I expected a couple of things. According to them, most of the students will be able to read and write English fairly well, but some might have difficulty speaking English. Also, they said that the Vietnamese students tended to cheat on tests by copying from one another. Some may even get up from their chairs and walk across the room to another student's desk to get or give help. I wondered if Vietnam's Confucian roots might explain, in great part, why the students behaved this way. Vietnam is a collectivist culture, like other Asian cultures, including Japan, Korea, and China, while individualism describes the culture of American society and Western Europe. Collectivists believe the community must work together, and they emphasize family and group goals, while Americans work as individuals, and compete with one another, sometimes at the expense of the group. However, that was not the case in the US military. In the military, we all had the same haircuts and dressed alike. We learned to operate as a team. We stayed in step. The military taught us to do what I was reading about in the academic literature on collectivism.

My syllabus outlined what we were to cover day by day, with a footnote indicating that I reserve the right to modify it during the semester to better meet the needs of the class. Since I had posted the syllabus online in advance of the first class, I was already handing out a revised syllabus in the first-class session. Day one, according to my revised syllabus, called for me to spend time introducing myself to the students and finding out a little bit about them (as a cohort, they already knew each other). On file with the university were both my résumé and curriculum vitae (CV). I provided both to the Hanoi MBA Program because the CV format did not include the depth of business experience I'd gained during the thirty-five years when I worked as a business professional, but the résumé format did. And though the résumé format was, in my judgment, more appropriate for business students, I decided to include my CV, not my résumé, with the syllabus because the CV made no mention of my years in the military.

After introducing myself, I reviewed the syllabus in some detail so that there would be no surprises. I peeked at the class roster and saw that one of the older gentlemen in the class was from South Africa, but I was the only Black person in the room. I asked for him by name. A White man answered and said that he was a diplomat with the South African embassy and discussed briefly what he did for the embassy. Also, I noted from the roster that a couple of the students were now in their fifties. If they are now in their fifties, they would have been at least teenagers when 'Nam ended. I looked around the room and tried to pick out the older students, but this time, before I could ask for a particular student to speak, a female student raised her hand and asked me the question I most feared: "Have you ever been to Vietnam before?" That question took me aback and made me realize that I was right in thinking that some of the people in Hanoi saw me for who I was, a 'Nam Veteran. I wondered if she had seen my résumé.

I answered her, saying bravely, "Yes, I was in Vietnam many years ago, but never to Hanoi," and I wanted to add, but didn't, that I had not seen Hanoi before, not even from the sky.

She paused slightly before acknowledging what I had said, and then in perfect English alleged, "You may have been the one who shot my uncle!" At that very moment, all of my greatest fears seemed to be realized, for she knew—the whole class now knew—that I had been an enemy combatant. Then she smiled, as if to suggest that she only wanted to let me know that she knew. My feelings were muddled. Was she someone, or was there someone else in the class, I should be concerned about?

I asked her for her name and for her to tell me a little bit about herself. She said her name was Zoom, and that she was an accountant for the government. I quickly went down the roster to find her because I wanted to make certain that I remembered which student, on paper, she was. I could not find her name on the roster. I asked her for her full name so I might be able to find someone with her last name and a first name Zoom. Zoom explained that her name is spelled Dung, pronounced *Zoom*. She went on to explain that, in the south of Vietnam, the letter y is pronounced as a z, and that in the north, the letter *d* is pronounced as z. Also, she explained that in the North, Vietnamese use six tones when they speak, whereas in the South only five tones are used. *And I thought learning proper English was tough*, I said to myself.

The first day of class was challenging, mostly because I did not feel well, and my students came to realized that. I had a cold.

One student went into the hall where break-time refreshments were kept, made me a cup of Vietnamese tea, and brought it into the classroom. As grateful as I was for the tea, I was even more appreciative for the kindness that she exhibited. The class knew I was an enemy combatant, and still they showed kindness and consideration. The whole class seemed concerned about my welfare. If I had been in the States, I would have thought that they just didn't want the class to be canceled, but here I sensed something very different. At 10:00 p.m., the class was finally over. It was dark, and it was time to head back to the Sunway.

Out of the building and down the stairs of the school building I went. I headed down the alley, but this time I was comforted by the fact that some of the people getting on their motorbikes, bicycles, and walking behind me were my students. I even observed two late-model SUVs (a Toyota and a GMC, I think), picking up students I recognized; and as I watched them being met, probably by a spouse, boyfriend or girlfriend, or sister or brother, my perception of Hanoi was beginning to change. I was starting to see Hanoi as a vibrant city, the capital city of Vietnam, and not as 'Nam's Hanoi.

I exited the alley and made a right onto Lò Đúc Street and headed toward Pham Dinh Ho Street. At the corner of Lò Đúc and Pham Dinh Ho was the same young man on his bike I'd noticed on my way to the school, but this time he was sleeping on the bike. He apparently had no place to stay other than on his vehicle, which he had leaning on the same street pole where it had been when I saw him the first time. He had some belongings, maybe everything he owned, on the bike with him. I guess it was the Hanoi version of sleeping in the car.

In the States, people sleeping overnight in cars or vans are considered homeless. His situation seemed much worse. He was more like the homeless person I would see sleeping in a public place in the States, with all of his or her belongings in a bag. I wondered if in Hanoi, as in the States, homeless people are seen as outcasts. I wondered if he was putting himself at risk by sleeping in the street. In the States, many cities prohibit sleeping, lying, sometimes even sitting too long in a public space. In fact, in some US cities, you are not allowed to sleep in your own car, and so, sleeping on a motorbike leaning on a pole would certainly be unlawful. Because of such state laws, a homeless person, at times, ends up being charged with a victimless criminal offense, which makes it even more difficult for him to escape his circumstances. Sadly, a large percentage of the homeless people are Vietnam Veterans, and many are that way because they were not able to successfully transition back into civilian life. Many suffer from PTSD that goes untreated.

I continued along Pham Dinh Ho to the hotel, which was just a short distance away. I called up to the room from the lobby and asked Jackie if she wanted to join me in the first-floor dining area for a quick bite. She agreed. I said "quick bite," but really, I meant, "I need a bite, quickly!" I was famished and needed something to bite on before I figuratively starved to death, so I was hoping Jackie wouldn't interpret my statement to mean that I wanted something insignificant.

As much as fifteen minutes passed, and no Jackie. Just as I started to call her again to prod her, she exited the elevator. The quick bite I ordered was a steak dinner, which included french fries, a side of broccoli, and a salad. And, of course, a small bowl of ice cream for dessert. It was as close to American cuisine as one could find on the menu. I was simply too hungry to experiment.

As I chomped down on the steak, I began to feel guilty because I'd previously judged Michael for his lack of interest in Vietnamese culture. I remember thinking at the time that, given an opportunity, I would absorb the Vietnamese culture until it inexorably seeped from my pores. However, dinner was not about my pores, it was about my stomach! It was about a small slice of culture ... Vietnamese food culture. Jackie had eaten dinner while I was teaching, so she decided to have just dessert. She ordered cheesecake, expecting something akin to a New York-style cheesecake. What she got amounted to a donut with a cheese sauce poured on top.

The next morning, we decided that after breakfast we would try to get a phone charger for our personal Verizon phones. The phone the university had provided could only be used to make local calls, and we'd mistakenly left our Verizon chargers at home. We made a few calls using our personal phones, but now the batteries were completely dead.

After breakfast we visited a number of shops in the Sunway Hotel neighborhood in hopes of buying a charger, but none of the stores carried one compatible with our phones. Apprehensively, we walked another few blocks away from the hotel, and finally, we spotted what appeared to be a phone store. As we had been primed to expect, the store did not carry a charger compatible with either of our phones, and the salesperson had no idea where we might buy one. A customer overhearing our conversation approached, saying repeatedly, "I take you! I take you!" Her English was just good enough for us to understand that she was offering to help us, and that her name was Anh. We thanked her and introduced ourselves.

Anh took us around the corner to a store, and she explained to the shopkeeper that we needed a charger that would work for our phones. The shopkeeper walked to the back of the store and began searching through a few boxes. After a short while, he pulled out a funny-looking device, which was, according to him and Anh, a charger. Anh gestured for us to remove the batteries from our phones, and the shopkeeper took the batteries and showed us how to use what was not the typical-looking phone charger, but a battery charger. Outstanding! It was perfect, especially since Jackie and I did not have the same type phones. Our batteries were different, and both were dead. The charger could be adjusted to fit various size batteries. While the battery was being charged, the charger would flash brilliant red, green, and yellow lights. A lot of things in Hanoi seemed to have a bling or flashy quality to them. Then, to our surprise, Anh began bargaining with the storekeeper on our behalf. When she was done, we purchased the universal cell phone battery charger for less than three dollars. We learned that day, bargaining was expected behavior in Vietnam.

Before parting ways, Anh told us that she was the owner of a bar and restaurant in Hanoi, and she gave us her card with the address of her place. She asked us to consider stopping in some evening. We now had an invitation from Arthur to join him for dinner and an invitation from Anh to come to her bar. We were becoming quite the socialites.

Thanks to Anh, our shopping excursion proved successful, but more importantly, we got a chance to greet, speak to, and meet a few of the people of Hanoi. We were beginning to get a sense for the social fabric of the city. Jackie said she believed the reason the Vietnamese treated us with such kindness was because they are mostly Buddhists and follow the principles of Confucius. Buddhists, she said, "are gentle, tolerant, generous, hospitable people." Also, she added, "Buddhists have great respect for older people, older folk like us, and for teachers, like you." However, contrary to Jackie's understanding, my 'Nam experience taught me that, Buddhists or not, they can be rough, tough, fierce fighters.

That evening, I was once again off to school. I had spent much of the day walking around Hanoi. The walk tired me, and I was still quite ill, coughing and sneezing a bit. And I was losing my voice. Immediately upon my arrival to the classroom, several students approached, offering me remedies for my cold. They brought me Vietnamese and Russian medicine, cold lozenges, and even tea to take back to my room, which underscored what my wife thought about the Vietnamese culture. I immediately

started sucking on a lozenge, which helped immensely and immediately, while thinking perhaps my wife had been right. The students were being very considerate and hospitable.

The class, comprised mostly of working professionals, was able to hold lively discussions on the leadership cases I had assigned for each evening. I participated just enough to keep the meaningful and lively discussions going.

After a couple of days of teaching, I became very comfortable being a professor of students of Hanoi, and so it was time to think about sightseeing and engaging in some social activities. I wanted very much to catch up with Arthur and Anh, who had graciously invited us to connect with them before we returned to the States.

Jackie wanted to take a tour of the city preferably by bus to learn more about Hanoi and what it had to offer. I had a more specific itinerary, and considered taking full advantage of my taxi voucher to see those places. I wanted to visit the Hanoi war museum and the Vietnam Museum of Ethnology, the Ho Chi Minh Mausoleum, the Trúc Bạch Lake (where John McCain had landed when his aircraft was shot down), and the Hỏa

Lò Prison (nicknamed the Hanoi Hilton, where McCain was a guest of the North Vietnamese for six years). All of the places I wanted to visit were in some way connected to my stay in 'Nam and I hoped Michael would agree to be our tour guide. Michael

and his Vietnamese wife Linh agreed to give us a personal tour; however, they did not want to take us to the military related places on my list, and Jackie had absolutely no interest in seeing the Hỏa Lò Prison. The day they took us out for a tour, we were treated to lunch at a restaurant that was maybe a block or so from the Hanoi Hilton. It was to be the closest I would get.

THE TOUR

By the middle of our second week in Hanoi, we had fully recovered from our colds, and decided that we should take a bus tour and catch some of the sites of Hanoi that was not covered by Michael's personal tour. We scheduled a tour that included most of the places I wanted to see with the notable exceptions of the Hỏa Lò Prison and the war museum. The tour bus picked us up at the Sunway early on a Friday morning. Our hotel was the first among several hotels scheduled for pickup, and so for us, the first forty-five minutes of sightseeing was along the streets of Hanoi as we went from hotel to hotel and stopped to pick up other tourists. Once the tour got truly underway, we stopped at a number of interesting places. We visited the

We listened to women playing Vietnamese music in his honor.

Temple of Literature and the home of Vietnam's first national university. We learned that the Temple of Literature was now about one thousand years old, and that it was once the residence of the disciples of Confucius. On the grounds was an altar to Confucius, and in one of the buildings we listened to women playing Vietnamese music in his honor. Confucius, is quoted as saying, "Music produces a kind of pleasure which human nature cannot do without."

Then the tour bus took us to the Vietnam Museum of Ethnology, which was high on my list of places to visit because of the many artifacts and exhibits it had exemplifying Vietnam's different ethnic groups, including Yards. The way Montagnards were disregarded in Vietnam was, for me, reminiscent of how some early "Americans," Native Indians and Blacks, were mistreated in the US. The Montagnards' tribal lands were taken, they were given no legislative representation, local magistrates treated them poorly, and they could not even teach their native languages in their schools. This sounded, at least on the surface, very much like the plight of Native Americans in the US. It was not until after the passage of the Native American Languages Act (1990) that Native Americans were free to communicate, educate, and assess their children in their native language. And the Yards, like Black Americans at the time of the US Civil War, were at the time of 'Nam fighting for civil rights, making the museum even more of an imperative.

The museum was being well-visited by Vietnamese schoolkids the day we were there, and the students expressed great interest in me ... I bet I was the museum's most popular exhibit that day. One student approached me to ask if I would take a picture with her. I agreed. Then her friends asked if they could join us for a picture. I took several pictures with them while Jackie watched. She was never asked to join us! I should have asked Jackie to join us for a picture, but didn't. Upon reflection, I suspect that they had not previously had the opportunity to meet and take a picture with a Black person. Surely, they know about Blacks from war stories, TV shows, movies, and of course, sports. It reminded me of my

interest in taking pictures with Native Americans when I traveled to the Philmont Scout Ranch in New Mexico.

On the grounds outside of the museum were exhibits of dwellings which were much like the dwellings I recall seeing in the Central Highlands of Vietnam. Jackie found them to be extremely interesting. She walked in and out of virtually every one, though she chose not to climb the nine-step ladder into the Tay stilt house because it would have required too much of her physically.

The exhibit that most caught my eye was that of figures of Montagnard men displayed naked—with large, erect phalluses—standing at attention and facing pregnant Montagnard women. I wondered if the exhibit could be a depiction of stereotypical Montagnard men; like the myth that Blacks are sex-crazed people with large appendages. The tour guide explained that the sexually explicit figures were symbols of fertility, which I believe was his way of saying that Montagnards are prolific. It also brought to mind a report that I'd read sometime after returning from 'Nam that said Montagnard women were being forcibly sterilized by the Vietnamese government.

Somewhat close to the huts at the Ethnology Museum was an outdoor puppet theater where we watched a water puppet show. Vietnamese water puppet shows date back to the 11th century. We learned that the puppets were controlled with bamboo poles hidden under the water. And as amazing and enjoyable

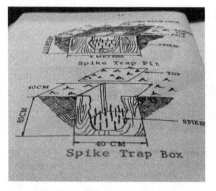

They would urinate or smear feces on the bamboo, camouflage it so that their enemy would unknowingly step on the bamboo spikes and possibly get an infection

as the show was, the idea of hidden bamboo poles was reminiscent of sharpened bamboo stakes placed at the bottom of a hole by the Viet Cong to wound their unsuspecting enemy. They would urinate or smear feces on the bamboo, camouflage it so that their enemy would unknowingly step on the bamboo spikes and possibly get an infection. After the puppet show we were off to the Ho Chi Minh Mausoleum, which was important to me because through my studies of Uncle Ho for class, I learned that immediately after World War II he proclaimed Vietnam's independence saying, "All men are born equal: the Creator has given us inviolable rights, life, liberty, and happiness!" (History.com Editors, 2020) Sounds familiar.

As we approached the mausoleum, I could see a very long line of people waiting to pass by the embalmed body of Ho Chi Minh. We had to walk a bit to find the end of the line and by then Jackie's weak back and her recently operated-upon knee were beginning to give her trouble, and so we decided not to enter the mausoleum and to wait seated on a bench near our bus. That way, we could easily board the bus and join the others for the next leg of the trip.

We sat, solemnly observing the people leaving the mausoleum. Observing people's reaction to the mausoleum was more important for me to see, I feel, than was the building and the tomb inside. Many of the visitors were looking down, and virtually everyone had a mournful demeanor. Many of the people appeared to be foreigners, and there were a great number of Asians … my guess is that most were Vietnamese. And many of the men leaving the mausoleum wore the uniform of the North Vietnamese Army. Some were visibly disabled, and they all seemed to have numerous medals on their chest. I wondered how many Americans each had captured, wounded, or even killed in 'Nam, and I contemplated what they might be thinking as they passed by me.

From the corner of my eye, I watched an amputee take a seat on the other end of my bench. He seemed weary; perhaps he was waiting for someone. I eventually looked his way and greeted him, saying, "Chào anh," which I understand to be hello to someone who appears to be older. I took Vietnamese lessons and learned a little Vietnamese while stationed in Pleiku, but I couldn't help but wonder if I had made a faux pas, like the one I'd made in the Hong Kong airport. I wondered if perhaps *xin chào*, (a more general and polite hello) would have been a more appropriate greeting. He responded as he rose and walked away. And though I didn't understand what he said, his demeanor, at least to my reading of it, suggested that I had not in any way offended him. I could not help but watch his gait as he walked away, while speculating about how he'd lost his leg. Then Dung's words began to march around in my head, "You may have been the one who shot my uncle!"

We then boarded the bus and headed for the Trúc Bạch Lake. The tour guide explained that it was there that, "the good citizens of Hanoi saved the life of the US presidential candidate John McCain," by pulling him safely from the water. Jackie was just as surprised as I was at this narration of the event. It seemed the tour guide was putting a "Buddhist spin" on it. Or was he? The way we remembered hearing the accounts of Senator McCain's plight was that he had been shot down by a missile and he parachuted into the Trúc Bạch Lake. We understand that the citizens of Hanoi did pull McCain to shore, but they then beat him from the pent-up anger that had built in them. They were angry about the tremendous devastation done to their city from repeated attacks by US planes like the one McCain flew. Placed near the lake was a monument commemorating the capture during the war of (who was now) US Senator McCain. It mentioned that his plane was one of ten aircraft shot down that same day.

As we sat waiting for the tour bus to take us back to the hotel, Jackie mentioned that she was going to ask the driver to reverse his route. She wanted our hotel to be the first stop after the tour, since before the tour, we had to sit patiently on the bus a long time while it picked up other tourists. I told Jackie that the driver probably had a set route and I doubted that he could take the liberty of changing it just because she asked, but she insisted on trying. When the bus arrived, Jackie approached the driver with her request while I proceeded to find seats for us in the middle of the bus. She spoke with the driver, and then with a big smile on her face, walked briskly toward me. "The driver agreed," she exclaimed. She was really ecstatic that he had said, "yes".

However, I cautioned her saying, "Remember before coming to Hanoi I told you that in some cultures, particularly in Asian cultures, "yes" can mean, "I understand," or it can be used simply to acknowledge what is being asked, not 'I will' or 'I agree'." Perhaps she had forgotten that, or maybe she'd remembered it intellectually but never really took it to heart. Even after I jogged her memory, she insisted that the driver had agreed, and she said that she would be extremely disappointed if he did not "keep his word." Her response would not be surprising to most Americans, because Americans tend to be relatively low-context, and in my view, ethnocentric. That is to say, we prefer direct, verbal contact and would rather not have to read between the lines or understand or depend on nonverbal clues (Loewy, D.

& Guffey, M. 2013). In America, "no" means "no"; "yes" means "yes". Even at home, cultural differences between Jackie and I would play out in much the same way.

The bus finally reached its first stop, and to me, there was no surprise. It was not the Sunway. Jackie became visibly upset and disappointed, but when we reached the second hotel and it, too, was not the Sunway, it infuriated her. I could hardly hold her in her seat! Luckily, I had taken the aisle seat so that she would have to circumvent me to get to the driver. As she began to settle down, she said repeatedly, "Yes means yes!" Her assertion was a stark reminder that information is not knowledge; information becomes knowledge only when one absorbs it to the point that it is as tacit and as familiar as, say, riding a bike.

Our tour of Hanoi would not be complete without visiting Hanoi's war museum in the Ba Dinh district (formerly the French Quarter) but the bus tour did not include the war museum. So, after breakfast on Thursday, we stopped by the hotel manager's desk to ask him about the museum and to have him call a cab to take us there. As soon as I mentioned the words "war museum," the manager corrected me, noting adamantly that, "Hanoi does *not* have a war museum. It is a military museum!" I found the fact that he would make this distinction fascinating. I recalled that, in the States, we have both war and military museums, and I had not previously thought about there being a difference between the two types. I became curious about the distinction. Intuitively, I felt the difference must be that a war museum commemorates a particular conflict while a military museum focuses on military services and military arms at various points in time. I thought about the Virginia War Museum, and I recalled that it displays uniforms and weapons from the Revolutionary War through 'Nam. If my thesis is correct, the Virginia War Museum would have been more appropriately named the Virginia Military Museum, since it does not memorialize a particular conflict. This would be consistent with the hotel manager's point that Hanoi's museum is a military museum … it does not cover just 'Nam. I found it fascinating that the manager in the high context culture that is Vietnam's, would make such a low context distinction.

I acknowledged the manager's correction by asking, "Would we be able to see captured US equipment from the Vietnam War at Hanoi's military museum?" I was careful not to stress the word "military" for fear that he might think I was being sarcastic and that question, I thought, would most certainly eliminate any doubt that I was a 'Nam Vet. For me, however, being able to even ask that question of a citizen of Hanoi was confirmation that I was getting stronger emotionally, and that I was moving further away from the dreadfulness of the war. Like an astute politician, the manager promptly changed the issue by asking for clarification of my question. "Do you mean the American war?" From his perspective, it was the American war. The manager explained further that his country had fought and won numerous wars. Most notably there was the First Indochina War with the French (1945-1954), and the Second Indochina War (1955-1975) with the US and its allies, which is commonly referred to as the Vietnam War. Perhaps I can rid myself of the stigma of being a "baby killer" by replacing my Vietnam Veteran t-shirts with ones that read "Indochina War II Veteran."

I should not have expected a direct answer to the question, "Would we be able to see captured US equipment from the Vietnam War at Hanoi's military museum?" And none was offered. Though we'd lost the War our primary objective may have been achieved, for with the exception of Laos and Cambodia, communism did not spread throughout the rest of Southeast Asia. And now Vietnam is doing extensive business with the United States.

Hanoi's Military Museum illuminated Vietnam's military history from before the heroic efforts of the Trung sisters, to the battles with the French and the US, and beyond. As I had expected, the museum displayed weapons used by both Vietnam and the US, as well as war photographs, captured fighter planes and helicopters, and various other captured US equipment. There was even a captured US Army tank. Also on display were Soviet fighter jets used against the US, with descriptions in English in all caps, which told of the particular plane. The description on one Soviet MIG read:

> RIGIMENT 921, DIVISION 371 OF THE VIET NAM
> PEOPLE'S AIRFORCE USED THIS MIG TO SHOOT
> DOWN 5 U.S. AIRCRAFT, INCLUDING A B-52 BOMBER
> WHICH WAS DOWNED BY PILOT PHAM TUAN ON
> THE NIGHT OF DECEMBER 27TH, 1972.

The description under another MIG credited that plane with having downed seven US Air Force planes. Captured helicopters, similar to the ones I'd flown on from time to time, were among the relics that brought 'Nam back to life for me. I remembered that, on May 12, 1970, commander Lieutenant Colonel Cole's helicopter was shot down near Pleiku, and on the same day, Major General Dillard and nine other Americans were killed when their helicopter was hit by enemy fire and crashed about ten miles southwest of Pleiku.

I was sent to Pleiku as a radio teletype team chief to replace a radioman for a unit that was losing a communications specialist from either rotation, serious injury, or death. Being a radioman was a very risky military occupational specialty (MOS). An example of a radioman's potentially hazardous duty, described in a report by *The Redstone Rocket*, elucidates this risk:

> Jim Shingleton was among 28 Soldiers that left Fort
> Ord, California, on Dec. 23, 1966, and arrived the next

day, Christmas Eve, in Vietnam. The newly graduated communications specialists landed in Pleiku and were then flown to base camp An Khe.

Shingleton, however, had gotten sick and missed the flight to An Khe. Within a week, he caught a helicopter there and learned that 26 of the original 28 were dead.

Such was the shortened life expectancy of radio telephone operators in Vietnam (Vaughn 2015).

I replaced an operator in headquarters and headquarters company (HHC) of the 20th Combat Engineer Battalion, a combat-ready unit ... thankfully, it was not infantry. Army communications training taught me all I needed to know about radio and radio teletype communications, but it did not teach me all I wanted to know about communicating with people in Vietnam who were not military. I wanted to know, not only about the techniques for talking among ourselves on the radio, but also about how to be an effective communicator with Vietnamese citizens. That required learning about Vietnamese culture. In my view, familiarizing oneself with the Vietnamese language, the dominant religions, and importantly, nonverbal communications, was all part of the job. In most countries, for example, nodding one's head up and down means yes, but there are countries where it means no. And in some countries, yes means simply, "I understand what you're asking." Vietnam happens to be one of those countries. I was able to take a Vietnamese language class given by the military before leaving for 'Nam, and I counted on the Army to provide tips on significant differences in our cultures, but I got little information before heading to Southeast Asia. After returning home, understanding cultural differences became really important to me in my time teaching as a business professor.

White skin is thought to be beautiful and is often thought of as symbolizing a person of a higher social class. In America, however, Whites will go into the sun to get a tan, which may suggest that one has leisure time to golf, play tennis and participate in other outdoor recreational activities. The Vietnamese also see white skin as signifying that one is of an upper class, but there people will cover up so that they will not get any darker; dark skin suggests a lower class, it says you may work in the field, as would a farmer. "I want my skin to be white because I think it is beautiful," says a 31-year-old woman working in Ho Chi Minh City, "But I also want to protect myself from the sun ..." (Rowse, 2003).

Prior to being stationed in Pleiku, I thought of Vietnam as being a mostly homogenous society of the Viet, or Kinh, ethnic group. On my flight from Biên Hòa to the Pleiku Air Force Base, I was awakened to Vietnam's true demographics. There were a number of dark-skinned people on the plane, dark like me, who would be dark even if they covered up from the sun. The country's demographics surprisingly seemed much like that of the US. The dark-skinned minorities of Vietnam are Montagnards (Yards). Yards fought with the French during the First Indochina War, and with the US against the Vietcong and North Vietnamese Army (though there were some in both conflicts who fought with the opposition). Yards would walk down the road in a single line, men followed by women. The women wore breechcloths and often nothing above the waist. The men wore loincloths and carried bows and arrows, and sometimes machetes reminiscent of Native Americans carrying knives and hatchets. Having grown up watching television shows about how American settlers had to protect themselves against Native Americans, I of course initially felt uneasy in the presence of Yards. And just as Native Americans were once considered savages, Yards suffer from that same sentiment.

And like the Indian tribes of California who ate meat, fish, and small animals (such as rats) for protein (Mullen 2003), Yards eat a similar diet. Each night, we would try to catch a rat or two in the tactical operation center (TOC), the battalion's primary communications bunker, to give to the Yards.

DINNER IS ON YOU

We made plans to meet Arthur at the Mediterraneo, an Italian restaurant on Nha Tho Street. While preparing to meet him, Jackie, who comes from an Italian and Irish background, and who really enjoys Italian cuisine, started questioning the wisdom of Arthur's choice of venue, thinking we were in Vietnam, not Italy or New York, nor even Delaware's Little Italy in Wilmington. Rhetorically, she asked, "Who would think of going to an Italian restaurant in Vietnam?" And mumbling to herself, she said quietly, "Westerners," and then crescendoed to say loudly, "and he highly recommends the place! Perhaps Arthur does not know good Italian cuisine, and like you," she continued reminding me of my earlier comment, "perhaps embracing other cultures, particularly others' food cultures, does not come easy." Jackie was right about one thing: the food I enjoyed most was based upon what I'd experienced growing up. Embracing other cultures, particularly others' food cultures, does not come easy; yet, I was open to learning about another food culture if it was slightly divergent from the tastes, likes, and expectations of my limited American palate.

I thought back to when my father brought home a pizza pie for the first time. At the time, there were no pizza restaurants in Harlem ... perhaps there were a few in East Harlem, but certainly none in a ten-block (half-mile) radius of where I lived. In New

York City, ten blocks is a long way, because very few people have cars, and even for those who do, driving can be a real chore. To travel ten blocks, one generally took public transportation, called a cab, or walked. Because Pop worked for the New York City bus company (as a diesel mechanic), and the garage he worked out of was in Spanish Harlem on the eastside, he could easily get a pizza. This day, he did. When he opened the pizza box, the pizza looked to me as if someone had regurgitated in the box. But if Dad, who was more tethered to his friends than his family, thought of us enough to bring it home, I would bravely try it. I tried it, and it was actually pretty good. Really good!

"Jackie," I said, "I really don't enjoy eating foods other than American, Mexican, Italian, and Asian cuisine. I do enjoy Chinese food, especially cashew chicken and General Tso's chicken. I also enjoy pepper steak and Szechuan chicken." *Back in 'Nam, the only time I ate Vietnamese food was when I was invited to have dinner with ROK (Republic of Korea) Soldiers with whom I was studying Taekwondo. I didn't like the food they ordered for me, but I ate it.Was I being ethnocentric?*

"And as you know," I continued, "I worked two weeks in Japan, and there I had some of the best Italian food I have ever eaten," I said with a grin. "It was at a jazz club in Tokyo." *I had just talked myself into thinking that I should not be so closed minded and be completely open to what Mediterraneo had to offer.*

And so, Mediterraneo it was. As it turned out Mediterraneo was, from my way of thinking, in the perfect location for an Italian restaurant for it was in view of St. Joseph's Cathedral. In Sicily, St. Joseph is considered by many as their patron saint, crediting him for preventing a famine in the Middle Ages. Patronizing Mediterraneo seemed most appropriate.

After a short time in the restaurant, Jackie expressed great satisfaction, noting that the ambiance seemed fitting and matched what she envisioned a good Sicilian restaurant in Italy to be like. And though her words may have been heartfelt, they were also to remind me that I had promised we would vacation in Italy someday. Adding to the mood was the restaurant's owner, Leonardo, who was from Italy, and who personally prepared the food that was as good as we had ever experienced in Italy … New York's Little Italy, that is.

We chatted with Arthur for several hours. Jackie mentioned that she was Italian on her dad's side, and that her mom and dad had eloped. They were not thrilled about having to elope, she said, but felt they had to do so because Jackie's maternal Irish grandparents were not happy about her mom marrying an Italian guy. She explained that her parents wanted to marry during a time in the US when Italian and Irish immigrants fought for jobs and housing, which often resulted in great physical conflicts between the two groups. Even as Jackie told the story, I realized that she knew much more about the relationship between her Irish and Italian parents, and how it affected our relationship, than she was mentioning.

Jackie knew that her paternal grandparents came from a long line of tailors, and they owned their own tailoring business. Her parents never felt financially insecure because Jackie's dad had acquired tailoring skills from his parents, skills that he could bank on. And because he was financially secure and comfortable with his own cross-cultural relationship, he was OK with Jackie and I being married. However, he recognized the hurdles we would face would be more challenging than the ones he had to confront when he'd married his Irish sweetheart. But still, he was to a great degree supportive of our union. Jackie's mother, Laura, however, was not at all ready to accept the idea of her daughter marrying a Black man. I did not get a chance to meet her because she was in the hospital in Florida, and I decided to wait until she was discharged before visiting with her. One day, she called to speak with Jackie. They spoke a long time and

Jackie decided to introduce us over the phone. I spoke briefly. She died the very next day... had I contributed to her demise?

Much has been written about the potentiality of relationships between people of African and Irish ancestry (e.g. *Irish Americans And Whiteness* 2023), and many Europeans considered the Irish to be just a small cut above enslaved black Africans. Perhaps this tainted Laura's view of our relationship. The Blacks and Irish were both considered by many, back in the day, to be less than intelligent, happy-go-lucky people with talents for music and dance.

Beginning to feel left out of the conversation, I jumped in saying, "Jackie, as an Irish-American, and me being an Afro-American, come from similar backgrounds of common struggles in the US." I mentioned that, "In the nineteenth century, for example, African Americans were often referred to as monkeys, while Irish-Americans were referred to as apes. Simianization, is something we have in common... we are cousins." *And laughing to myself I thought, but there is no incest going on here.* To not be rude, I asked, "Arthur, please tell us a little bit about yourself," thinking Arthur is of Italian descent and hoping we had not said anything that he could have taken offense to.

For someone we had just met, he made us feel really comfortable about opening up to him. He seemed mainly interested in how Jackie and I became a couple, particularly after we told him we had been together for thirteen years. I told the story of our meeting at Salomon, the Wall Street brokerage firm, and spoke about the many challenges we had faced over the years as an interracial couple. He seemed uncomfortable about discussing what amounted to racism, and when I mentioned that we had met at work, Arthur took the opportunity to shift the conversation away from the trials and tribulations of intercultural marriage to talk about work, his work. But I was not willing to let this work discussion go on because Jackie and

I had taken the risk of investing so much of ourselves in our conversation that I wanted a return on that investment, and so I asked, "So, what is your background, Arthur?" He said he was Irish, like Jackie's mom. I was wrong, he was not Italian as I had thought. He didn't have blue or green eyes and reddish hair, but he was Irish. Then there was a short moment of silence. I could not help but think that he shared Laura's view on our marriage. After a few minutes, I mentioned again that I only had the memory of a quick telephone conversation with Jackie's mom.

By the conclusion of the evening, we had come to know a little more about Arthur and had come to accept that Mediterraneo was the fine Italian restaurant that Arthur had billed it to be … and he paid the tab, to boot. That made an already superb evening even more enjoyable, at least for Jackie and me. Our dinner conversation was perhaps a bit awkward and maybe a little inconsiderate to Arthur, but it gave us the chance to release much of the agony that had unknowingly built in us as an interracial couple. "Supportive companions" was the phrase that we coined early in our marriage to describe the relationship that we had and must continue with going forward.

After returning to the hotel, we sat around in the lobby relaxing. I had a couple of glasses of wine, and Jackie had a few Diet Cokes. After some time, we were greeted and joined by the hotel's general manager, George Teh, and then by one of the sales representatives for the hotel, Nham Phuong Hoa. They spoke proudly about Sunway, noting that it was one of Hanoi's best hotels and a leading hotel and resort for Asia, serving Cambodia, Malaysia, and Vietnam. Jackie and Phuong Hoa immediately connected when the rep mentioned that she had a ten-year-old daughter.

The fact that hotel management would seek me out was proof, I thought, that I was finally accepted, maybe not for who I am, but for the potential business I might bring. We talked about how our days went, and Phuong Hoa asked if we would have dinner with her and her daughter. I wondered if I was again being put on exhibit, as I had been at the museum. A number of possibilities came to mind, but I settled on the idea that perhaps she'd picked up on the fact that Jackie loves children, and having her daughter join us was her way of strengthening ties with us, and ultimately, getting more business from the university. We agreed to join her and her daughter for dinner at the Sunway the following evening.

GETTING TO KNOW YOU

The Sunway Hotel attracts its guests, mostly businessmen and women, from around the world, and so Jackie and I did not attract particular attention. Yet, at dinner that night, Phuong Hoa and her ten-year-old daughter Yen, who looked to be no older than six, seemed to be very uncomfortable with Jackie and me. Phuong Hoa explained that her daughter was very bashful and had not had the opportunity to speak with foreigners very much, to which Jackie commented, "We probably look like monsters to her." I had been called all kinds of things before, but never a monster … and certainly not by any of my wives! Jackie was wife number three (*vợ ba*), but that's another story. I was now beginning to recall the few Vietnamese words I'd learned, and I remembered the word for wife is *vợ*. I supposed *vợ ba* to mean "wife three," or "third wife," since *ba* was the word for three … how awkward it would be, I contemplated, if Yen understood what was being said.

I decided I might ease the tautness of the conversation by offering to play a game with Yen, and so I asked, "Yen, do you know how to count in English?"

"Yes, I do," she responded in very good English. Now I knew for certain that Yen could speak English fairly well, and yes meant yes.

Hearing her speak in English made me wonder if she knew the word "monster" in the context that Jackie had meant it.

Maybe she did see Americans, us, as relatively tall, overweight, wicked people—monsters. Undoubtedly, she has heard horror stories about the "evil Americans" and what we did to Hanoi and Haiphong during the American war. The Air Force and the Navy had devastated those places with their bombing operations: Rolling Thunder, Linebacker, and Linebacker II. Unlike the Air Force and Navy, the Army did not go into North Vietnam to kill the people there. At least not as far as I knew. We were different; we were Army. Our job was to help the Vietnamese people, those under the newly formed South Vietnamese government, remain safe and free from Communism. Was that not why we were there? *Being honest with myself, I must admit we wanted to attack the North. I recalled how my buddies and I would sit around in our bunker, saying to one another, "We should attack and destroy Hanoi so we can get the war over with and we can get the hell out of this place."* And now I'm having dinner in North Vietnam with a Communist family.

I looked closely at Yen as I told her that I knew how to count to 999 in Vietnamese. (Had I not forgotten the word for "thousand," I would have been able to count to just under a million). And I suggested that we play a game whereby I would first give her a number in Vietnamese for her to translate into English, and then she would give me a number in English that I would translate into Vietnamese. I structured the game so that I would have to speak Vietnamese and she would have to speak English. Apparently, she did not understand me because she had a look of puzzlement.

As I continued to stare at Yen, I could not stop reliving, in my mind, bygone war memories. Hadn't I been in Vietnam the first time to help the Vietnamese in the South keep the Communists in the North, the Democratic Republic of Vietnam, from taking over, like we'd tried to help the South Koreans keep the Communist North Koreans, The Democratic People's

Republic of Korea, from taking over? Vietnam and Korea, using the same terminology used by the US (democratic republic) to explain our government is very confusing.

> The United States government is a complex entity known as a *democratic republic*. This essentially means that the government operates on the principles of both a republic and a democracy. In other words, the nation functions upon principles that are common in both republics and democracies (Childs 2018).

It begs the question: *what was the fight all about?* I think we find the answer in Shakespeare's Romeo and Juliet: "What's in a name? That which we call a rose by any other name would smell just as sweet." The naming of things is irrelevant. *Is Communism just another name?*

Sitting across the table from a young "North" Vietnamese schoolgirl and her mother, and truly enjoying their company evoked the sad remembrance that, from the time 3,500 US Marines of the 3rd Marine Division arrived in Vietnam to the War's end, we lost over fifty-eight thousand men and women, some my friends. Even more to my chagrin was the fact that the US lost some forty thousand GIs in Korea in less than half the time, only to have it end as a stalemate. Upon reflection, I am convinced that war, cold or hot, is the only "game" one might engage in where a tie or stalemate is worse than losing, because normalized relations seem achievable only after a victor is recognized. The Korean War ended in a stalemate, and though our relationship with the South Koreans, for whom we fought, appears to have only strengthened since the war, antipathy with the North continues. We lost in Vietnam and now have normalized relations. Why not find a way to normalize relationships before the shooting begins?

My thoughts then turned to how an American soldier's compassion and love for children and respect for elderly people could cost him his life, because the VC (Viet Cong) would use our kindheartedness strategically against us. I recalled how some of the guys took an ambulance and turned it into what they called Alice's Restaurant, named after the anti-war song by Arlo Guthrie, "Alice's Restaurant." The *Restaurant* would go from village to village giving away treats, mostly candy. Then, one day, someone dropped a hand grenade with a rubber band wrapped around its handle into the fuel tank of Alice's Restaurant. Once the gas ate away at the rubber band just enough, the grenade's handle released and the grenade exploded. We think it might have been a kid who'd dropped the hand grenade into the fuel tank, because the Soldiers would guard against this happening, and only a kid would be allowed close enough to the vehicle to have done this. Alice's Restaurant was no more, and our empathy for the South Vietnamese, the people we were there to help achieve liberty and democracy, began to fade.

Also, I remembered being warned when I first arrived in Pleiku not to give a lift to any Vietnamese—soldier or civilian, young or old—no matter how desperate they seemed. Yet, I found it extremely difficult to pass by old women or a woman with children struggling down the road. And I recalled how I would think it unfriendly, even disrespectful, to treat South Vietnamese Soldiers with whom we fought alongside, as not being worthy of the same decency I would give an American, Aussie, or ROK soldier. How could I follow such a warning? *I would definitely pick them up, I thought, and give them a ride.* In fact, I would feel even safer knowing that there was another warm body in the vehicle to warn me and fight with me if the "shit hit the fan." That was until it actually happened. It was announced one morning that a member of the unit had been shot in the back of the head by an older Vietnamese woman he'd picked up on the road. War has a culture, and to evaluate one's thinking and actions using solely the norms and values of one's homegrown culture can cost a life, which may be your own.

My attention returned to Yen, and I could not help but notice once again that her English was rather good, especially for a young "North" Vietnamese girl, and yet I didn't think that she quite understood the game I was proposing we play. Her mother intervened and explained to her—in Vietnamese, of course—what I was suggesting we do ... well, I guess that is what Phuong Hoa was saying; after all, I could not know for certain because I didn't understand a word she said. As her mother spoke, a big smile grew on Yen's face, seemingly signifying that she not only understood her mother but also that she was interested in doing it. Then her mother turned to me with a smile of approval. What a healthy reminder that kids are kids, and mothers are mothers the world 'round.

Looking into the eyes of a young North Vietnamese schoolgirl made my mind hold onto the guilt I felt deep inside. My thoughts would not let me be completely free from the past as I thought about the bombings of Hanoi and Haiphong and the Mỹ Lai village massacre, juxtapose the Alice's Restaurant incident.

I was "in-country," as we would say it to mean in Vietnam, when in 1970, "the world" (that is, anywhere but Vietnam) came to find out that a group of US Soldiers killed as many as five hundred men, women, and children of Mỹ Lai. *That was an Army unit, but it was not us, I kept hearing me tell myself.* Not only were the men with whom I served not baby-killers (as many of us were called when we finally got back to the "world," because of unfortunate events like Mỹ Lai), but we'd suffered casualties at the hands of villagers who were indoctrinated by the VC to think we were. In 'Nam, there were people of all ages and genders who wanted to kill us. I looked at Yen and Phuong Hoa, and the gleam in Yen's eyes and her mother's smile as the cause for the return of the same ambivalent feelings I'd had about the war.

I was anxious for Yen and I to begin playing, not just for Yen's sake, but for mine as well. I truly enjoyed playing with kids, besides which, I wanted to know if I could recall and speak the little Vietnamese that I'd learned nearly five decades ago. I expected that I could speak at least well enough for Yen to understand some words.

I started by saying, "Hai." Yen replied, "Two." Both Phuong Hoa and Yen seemed impressed that I could say two in Vietnamese correctly. Jackie was not surprised because she had heard me speak a few Vietnamese words back in the States to operators in nail salons. Then it was Yen's turn to give me a number in English that I would translate into Vietnamese. Once again, her mother, Phuong Hoa, had to intervene for her to understand. And as before, Yen smiled. At first, she went easy on me, giving me the number three, which I properly translated. "*Ba*," I said. I continued by giving her a number in Vietnamese for her to translate. Then she gave me a number in English for me to translate. We continued taking turns, with each iteration getting more and more challenging. I not only had to know the number in Vietnamese, but I also had to say it correctly. As the game progressed, we gained respect for each other's abilities, and we seemed to become more and more competitive as we took turns. Yen had no plans of losing. She had Trung sister-like persistence and determination. I could feel through her the competitiveness, strength, and determination of our former enemy. It is said that the United States won every major battle in Vietnam, but we failed to win over the hearts and minds of the Vietnamese people with our program of pacification. As my father would tell me often, "The only person who can pick your pocket is someone you let get close." The Vietnamese apparently understood that.

I was able to get close to Yen and Phuong Hoa, but I had no intention of picking their pockets, literally or figuratively, but to develop a friendship based upon mutual respect and admiration. That is what I observed in Hanoi: friendship between the people of Vietnam and the US, mostly in the way we appeared to be doing business with one another. The US's pacification program during the Vietnam War sought to develop a friendship of utility where we, and the people in the villages of Vietnam, would benefit. It was to be a quid pro quo whereby, in return for the protection of rural areas from the Vietcong, the Saigon government would get political and administrative support. However, we continued to use napalm, often hitting civilians, and our search-and-destroy missions turned many villagers against us. Soldiers knew somehow that God was on their side and would sometimes pray for His protection. Now that we lost the War, I can see God and Buddha collaborating, *and I laughed to myself as we continued to play*, and Yen and her mother can now see Jackie and me not as ogres, but as friends. We had come to appreciate that we are all children of Buddha and God.

"Twenty-five," said Yen. And I responded, "Hai mươi năm." To which Yen indicated that I was wrong. "Wrong?" I said. I could not imagine why that would be wrong. *Hai* is two, *mươi* is ten, and *năm* is five. Two times ten, plus five, is twenty-five. Suddenly, I could visualize the words *hai mươi lăm* stamped adjacent to twenty-five dollars on my passport, the fee I'd paid to come into Hanoi. I immediately offered hai mươi lăm as my new answer and got a big smile of approval from Yen. I began to accept that there are exceptions in the Vietnamese language, as there are in English. What a disappointment! I thought back to what my ninth-grade teacher once asked me: "How could you be so good at math and not understand English grammar?" To which I replied, "Math makes sense and has fewer exceptions to the rules than English." I learned to count in Vietnamese because it made sense to me.

Then, it was my turn to give a number in Vietnamese to Yen. "Bảy muối," I said, thinking I was saying seventy. Phuong Hoa and her daughter both laughed. I think they knew I was attempting to say seventy, but obviously, I'd gotten that wrong too. I thought for certain I knew bảy muối to mean seventy, because in Vietnamese, seventy is simply seven (*bảy*), ten (*muối*), or is it? Phuong Hoa very politely explained that muối means salt, and that the word for ten is mươi, acknowledging *bảy mươi* was the word for seventy. As she spoke, I could hear a very, very, slight difference in the pronunciations of the two words muối and mươi, but I had great difficulty in saying ten correctly. I tried over and over to say bảy mươi (seventy) properly, but what came out again and again was bảy muối (seven salts). I guess we have more in common than I'd first realized; both languages can be difficult to learn. As I continued to struggle to say the two words, both Yen and her mother said that my pronunciation was getting better, but I had real doubts. I thought back to when Jackie and I were in search of a phone charger, and how Jackie made note that day that the Vietnamese people were treating us so kindheartedly. She said that she believed that they did so, in part, because of our age and because of their culture. The Vietnamese, she said, "show great respect to the elderly people, and we are getting up there in age." Getting up in age? I told her to speak for herself. As far as Yen and her mom were concerned, I thought that perhaps they appreciated my effort and desire to learn their language. Most importantly, we had great fun, Yen and I, as did Jackie and Phuong Hoa as they watched us. By the end of the evening, Jackie and I had two new comrades in spirit in Communist Hanoi. Yen won the game, but we won over the hearts and minds of a young Vietnamese girl and her mother.

BORN INTO A UNION

One morning, Nita awoke too sick to get out of bed to go to the neighborhood butcher; she wanted to get a chuck steak for dinner. She sent me. I was maybe a nine-year-old fourth-grader at the time. When I returned from the butcher, I marched proudly into her room, and with the meat in hand, I headed right to her bedside. She quickly looked at the meat and then, to my great disappointment, told me the meat was bad. It was so bad that she immediately got up out of her sick bed, put her hand on my back as if to say it is OK, and together we paraded back to the butcher to return the meat. She confronted the butcher, saying: "And you're Black like me. Take that meat home to your wife because your dog won't eat it."

Even as young as I was, I understood the subtleties of what was going on … well, maybe it was not so subtle, and I learned two very important lessons from the experience. First, I learned how to pick out a good piece of chuck steak, or at least how to identify a bad piece of meat. It was a lesson that has served me well my whole life. More importantly, it was my introduction as to how individuals are targeted because of one or more demographic characteristics, such as race, age, sexual orientation, and the list continues. I am sure I was targeted primarily because of my age, but there may have been other factors, such as gender and race, even though the butcher was of the same gender and race. I was also introduced to the idea that Blacks were duty bound to care for each other. "*And you're Black like me*," has resonated with me since. That day, I came to understand from my mother's behavior and sarcastic words that Blacks were born into a "union" (something my dad would say about women), which would bond us together as we advocated for our needs: physiological well-being, safety, love and belonging, esteem, and self-actualization; Maslow's hierarchy of needs (Maslow 1943).

The way I think about Maslow's three lower-level needs (physiological well-being, safety, love and belonging) is that they are human rights as much as they are needs. They comprise the rights one should get for just being alive (HUSL Library 2023). In his article, *Debate on Human Rights vs Human Needs*, Manuel Solis expresses concern about the United Nation's use of the term "human need" rather than "human right" in their call for universal access to sustainable modern energy services.

> A 'human needs' approach appeals to charity, while a 'human rights' approach translates need into a matter of entitlement with dignity (Solis, 2014).

In my view, Maslow's two higher needs: esteem and self-actualization fall into the category of rights, not human rights but civil rights. Unlike Maslow's lower-level needs, esteem and self-actualization are the rights of an individual to pursue personal growth and achievement and to endeavor as individuals to reach one's full potential. The butcher who would deny me, and thus my family, the basic physiological human need of edible food, a human right, was also robbing me of self-esteem, a civil right. "Civil rights are rights that one obtains by being a legal member of a certain political state" (HUSL Library 2023). Title II of the Civil Rights Act of 1964 reads in part:

You cannot be treated differently by a place of public accommodation because of your race, color, religion, or national origin (Your rights under Title II - united states department of justice).

Decades before the Civil Rights Act of 1964, Maslow recognized the importance of social needs: love and belonging, and postulated that meeting the hierarchy of needs is made easier when one lives in a fair and just society (Spagnoli, 2014). Unfortunately, the American society, back in the day, was not fair because it gave preference to Whites and lighter-skinned Blacks, and to taller people, regardless of gender or race. And this appears to be the case even today (Altitude Life Hacks 2019). Ironically, while Blacks have benefited from being light-skinned, Whites sometimes did what they could to become darker.

Nita was light-skinned and rather tall for a woman, and she was well aware of the fact that light-skinned Blacks receive preferential treatment. Some would say, "Nita could pass." And while many Blacks would see this as a compliment, for Nita, it was not a virtue. She did not feel that one must have White, European attributes to be considered worthy. Thus, if there is a third lesson I could learn from my experience at the butchers, it is "Keep vigilantly aware of people's attitudes and behavior toward you, even if they appear to be of the same 'union'."

Discrimination is systemic. Nita and Big Ralph, as our friends always called my dad, exemplified this to me by their feelings and treatment of our foster brothers and sisters. Big Ralph, who was very dark-skinned, appeared to gravitate toward foster kids of very light skin. I believe this was because of the benefits he felt awaited them in our society; benefits that he could not himself enjoy. Nita, on the other hand, seemed to give greater emotional backing to the darker-skinned foster kids who, I believe, she felt were truly in need of her support if they were to make it in this country.

I recall Nita commenting about Barbara, noting that she was definitely the darkest of all the foster kids she'd ever nurtured. Ralphy and I were about eight years older than Barbara, so Nita had no reservation in saying in our presence when Barbara was not around that "Barbara has very little chance of being adopted because she is just too dark." Consequently, of all the many kids my parents reared into adulthood, they adopted only one, Barbara; although dad's favorite foster kid was Beverly. Beverly's skin tone was nearly White. And as Nita predicted, Beverly stayed with us only a short time, maybe a year or possibly two, for she was quickly adopted. James Baldwin explains:

> You were born where you were born and faced the future that you faced because you were Black and for no other reason. The limits of your ambition were, thus, expected to be set forever. You were born into a society which spelled out with brutal clarity, and in as many ways as possible, that you were a worthless human being. You are not expected to aspire to excellence: you were expected to make peace with Mediocrity (Baldwin 1963).

During slavery days, plantations in the South would divide slaves into two groups—field slaves and house slaves—and would socially isolate the groups both physically and psychologically, with slaves working in the house considered the privileged social class. Often, they would be given the benefit of an education and more prestige. Female house slaves generally worked in close proximity to their slave owners and were sometimes taken as mistresses or raped by their owners (Densu, 2023). This separation—field and house—perhaps explains, at least in part, society's attitude toward people of darker skin hues. Growing up, I would hear, to my chagrin, a Black person characterized as a "house nigger." Senate Majority Leader Harry Reid, in 2008, remarked privately that Obama, as a Black candidate, could be successful because he was "light-skinned" and had "no Negro dialect," unless he chose to speak that way. Senator Reid did apologize, saying:

> I deeply regret using such a poor choice of words. I sincerely apologize for offending any and all Americans, especially African Americans for my improper comments (Zeleny 2010).

Colorism, is a term coined by Pulitzer Prize winner and author Alice Walker (circa 1982). It is a disease, just as some would say racism is a mental illness (Bell 2004), except with colorism one discriminates within their own race based on skin tone. Growing up, and for as far back as I can remember, all of us seemed to understand the notion of colorism. I can remember as a kid hearing a song that reflects its essence. Sadly, I believe I, too, at a very young age, sang the song, not understanding its implication:

> If you're black, stay back;
> If you're brown, stick around;
> If you're yellow, you're mellow;
> If you're white, you're all right.
> (Burnett 2011)

After the Civil War White landowners continued to control the Black labor force in much the same way they did during slavery. Black Codes were enacted to limit the economic activity of Blacks. In South Carolina, for example, a Black person could work only as a farmer or servant unless they paid an annual tax of $10 - $100. Ultimately, Blacks began to migrate from the South to cities in the North, Midwest and West. Some six million Blacks left the South between 1916 and 1970. It was called the Great Migration. About 200,000 Blacks moved into Harlem by the 1920s, which was at the time a White community (History. com Editors, 2010b).

A Black person traveling in the south in the 1930s and even today puts himself in jeopardy regardless of mode of transportation. On March 25, 1931 nine young men ages thirteen to nineteen were traveling by rail in a boxcar when they were removed from the train in Paint Rock, Alabama and taken to jail for allegedly assaulting a group of White men who were also on the train. When authorities learned that there were also two White women on the train, though in a different boxcar, authorities in Paint Rock upgraded the charges to rape. And though there was no evidence of rape presented, within three days the young men were tried for assault and rape. This case is known as the Scottsboro case (Kelley 1990, 78,79; *ACLU history: The tragedy of the scottsboro boys* 2010, 79; Mays, J & Jaffe, R. 2014).

The communist party came to the youngsters' aid and the case received international attention. On April 12, thirteen thousand people protested in Cleveland, and the next day twenty thousand people assembled in New York City. Unfortunately, eight of the nine youngsters were found guilty by all White juries. Found guilty without evidence proving their guilt. The eight were sentenced to death by electric chair (Kelley 1990, 78,79). Numerous organizations offered to help with their defense and ultimately, they were spared from execution; however, they had to spend many years in prison. In 2013, The Alabama Legislature, "passed a resolution declaring all nine Scottsboro Boys to be innocent" (Mays, J & Jaffe, R. 2014).

Victor Hugo Green, a Harlem postal carrier came up with the idea of publishing a guide to help Black travelers stay out of harm's way by providing a directory of where to eat and stay. He named his travel guide *The Green Book*. The first publication of the guide was in 1936. Hugo was inspired by a similar guide used by Jewish people published earlier (Andrews, 2017). *The Green Book* proved essential for Black travelers to find businesses, eating places and even gas stations, that would serve them. Few people, outside of the Black community, had ever heard of The *Green Book* until the film Green Book directed by Peter Farrelly and starring Viggo Mortensen and Mahershala Ali came out in 2018.

While at work at Salomon Brothers one day in 1989, it came to my attention that a fellow employee, Trisha Meili, who often jogged in Central Park had been attacked, beaten and raped. Five Black and Hispanic youngsters ages fourteen to sixteen were interrogated by police for at least seven hours without a parent or lawyer present. The interrogation led to an admission of guilt though the DNA from the semen didn't match any of the boys (*Central Park five: The true story behind when they see us* 2019). I was one of a few Blacks working for Salomon at the time and the case made for an uncomfortable work environment. A number of employees would spend much of their day discussing the Central Park Jogger case and what should be done to the five boys, while seemingly trying to keep their discussion out of earshot. From what I could hear, there seemed to be no consideration for the possibility that the boys might be innocent ... I guess not unexpected given they admitted to the crime. Of course, being Black, I had my doubts.

Thirteen years later Matias Reyes admitted to the attack and sexual assault and said he'd acted alone. His DNA matched that found at the crime scene, and since the Statue of Limitations had run out, Reyes was never prosecuted (*Central Park five: The true story behind when they see us* 2019).

In a 1924 article on racism and lynching, Ho Chi Minh wrote:

> It is well-known that the Black race is the most oppressed and the most exploited of the human

family. It is well-known that the spread of capitalism and the discovery of the New World had as an immediate result the rebirth of slavery. What everyone does not perhaps know is that after sixty-five years of so-called emancipation, American Negroes still endure atrocious moral and material sufferings, of which the most cruel and horrible is the custom of lynching (Haiphong, 2022).

On April 26, 2018, The National Memorial for Peace and Justice in Alabama opened to the public. The museum's exhibits are dedicated to the legacy of enslaved Black people who were terrorized and some even lynched.

LOVE IS FOR THE BIRDS

Nita was certainly no Pollyanna, and when I asked my parents about my background, they understood totally that I was not just asking about my background, but theirs as well. And for some reason, I felt awkward asking. And I got no answer other than that my paternal parents came to the US from Trinidad through Canada. You would think that I had asked them about sex, a taboo subject in our home, though Nita would at times joke about it, but that was as far as it went.

When I did get the courage to ask Nita about sex, she sent me to Big Ralph. A mistake, but I went to Dad, and he responded by first asking me rhetorically, "So, you want to know about the birds and the bees?" Then he said, "Be wise, love is for the birds." And yet, I felt more comfortable asking them about sex than about their backgrounds. Sex talk put me on the spot, while it seemed that talk about their backgrounds made me feel as though I was putting them on the spot. I continued with a few penetrating questions.

Ultimately, Nita said she did not really know her mother but she knew of her. The one thing that she did pass along to my brother Ralph and me was that her mother was the first female taxi driver in New York City. More recently, I read that Gertrude Hadley Jeannette, an African American woman, got a taxi license in 1942 and is recorded as the first female licensed taxi driver in the city. We were made to understand that our mother's mother was driving a cab well before 1942, which is a real possibility since metered cabs have been operating in New York City since 1907 and many of the cabs were being operated illegally. It was not until 1937 that a taxi license was needed in New York City under the Haas Act (Gelder, 1996). Consequently, Gertrude Hadley Jeannette may have been the first Afro-American woman to get a taxi license, but our mother's mother may have been the first female taxi driver. Who knows for certain? Regardless, Ralphy and I held on to this story because it is one of the few stories we have about our maternal grandmother. The one story we were told about our biological paternal grandfather was that, soon after my grandparents reached New York, my grandfather was able to find work, but soon afterwards, got an arm caught in a machine, which took his life. Big Ralph believes that someone arranged for him to lose his life by putting his arm into the machine.

Nita recalled being raised in New York and going to junior high school in Harlem, on 136th Street and Convent Avenue. The school was named after Harriet Beecher Stowe, a Black woman, and the author of *Uncle Tom's Cabin*. I remember Nita searching for her own birth certificate, not in some dresser drawer, but by contacting the health record bureaus of different cities: New York, Philadelphia, and Baltimore. She was not sure in which of these cities she had been born. I often wondered if my mother had been homeless, or a foster child. Was she the offspring of an escaped slave?

> Northern slave owners had little interest in family formation among slaves. The nature of urban life and small-farm production made large workforces untenable and unnecessary. While the plantation master approved of, oversaw, and often arranged

marriages among his slaves, the Northern master discouraged marital union and dissolved existing bonds by separating husbands and wives (Hallam).

Many of the slaves who escaped from Southern slave masters found their way to Philadelphia, Baltimore, or New York, where they could assimilate with free Blacks. These were the very cities where my mother had searched for her birth certificate. Was slavery on Nita's mind and the reason she did not know much about *our* roots? Were our forefathers slaves? Eventually, Nita obtained a copy of her birth certificate—from Baltimore, I believe—which to my way of thinking did not change the narrative that she was possibly a descendant of slaves. Slavery ended officially in 1865, and she might have been born a free person. Actually, I prefer the term *liberated person* because, though she would have been free from arbitrary and unreasonable restraint, she would still have been like the bird in the gilded cage. She would not have been completely free to fulfill her desires or seek Maslow's higher-level needs of self-esteem and self-actualization. She would have not been free in a county that legalized racial segregation from the post-Civil War era until around 1968, and beyond.

What I didn't understand was, "Why I had such an intense curiosity about where I came from?" I had two brothers, Ralph (little Ralph or Ralphy) and Bill. Ralphy and I met Bill when he returned from the Air Force in the very early 1960s. He was a stepbrother from my mother's first marriage, and an older brother and he made sure we respected that fact. He and Big Ralph were close, much closer than Ralphy or I were with Big Ralph. Nita made certain of that! We were not encouraged to hang out with Big Ralph or Bill because she feared that we would be introduced to some bad habits. Bill died around 1974.

The more I learned about my family, the more I wanted to know, and the more I realized I didn't know. My inquisitiveness paralleled that of my foster siblings, some of whom knew more about their backgrounds than I did about my own. Like them, I wanted a stronger sense of family, and I think as much as I enjoyed having my foster sisters and brothers around, my sense of family was actually weakened as one after another foster child joined us for only a short time and then left. The hallmark of civil rights is belonging ("Civil Rights. Community. Movement." 2020), and belonging, in my view, must start with family. Slavery denied us family, and Jim Crow denied us a sense of belonging... denied us the feeling of being more than a provisional member of the society. Nita was wise enough to know this, but she had no family to offer other than my siblings and foster brothers and sisters who are all considered full members of the family.

Having strong, close relationships among family and friends has always been vitally important to me. Growing up, I saw Harlem as a thriving, high-context collectivist community in a low-context, individualistic country. Of course, I was not able to put my impression of Harlem into words back then, but I did sense it. In any event, let me explain what I learned over the years as to why I might have felt this way.

Anthropologist Edward T. Hall formulated a cultural construct in which he outlined three cultural dimensions: context, space, and time. Context refers to whether information in a given culture has to be explicitly communicated or can be understood implicitly. In a high-context society, information need not be explicit to be effectively communicated, while in a low-context one, providing details so that the information is well-understood is expected (Loewy, D. & Guffey, M. 2013). Also, high-context cultures tend to be more collectivistic while people in low-context cultures value personal achievement and are individualistic. Individualism versus collectivism, is used to help understand the differences in cultural context across societies.

Blacks born in my day and earlier learned to communicate implicitly. Most African cultures are said to be high-context, and furthermore, I would postulate, because of slavery, Blacks in America had to communicate implicitly. As I got older, I noticed that Blacks tended to acknowledge each other's presence even when we did not personally know each other, where as a youngster, I would do it and not realize it. It was a tacit behavior. Even today, it seems to me that Blacks born in the sixties and earlier tend to acknowledge each other instinctively. Jackie would often ask me questions like, "Where do you know him from?" or "How do you know her?" My answer was most often the same, "I don't know him/her."

I would see cultural differences play out as I traveled by subway from Harlem to lower Manhattan to my first real job, which was before I was drafted. I worked as a computer programmer/ analyst for the American Book Company on 5th Avenue near 10th Street. To get there, I would catch the subway at the 135th Street and Lenox Avenue (now Malcolm X Boulevard) station in Harlem and ride it to 14th Street. From there, I would walk. On the train, Blacks would greet one another, and to my point, even when we didn't know each other. But as the express train pulled out of 125th Street, I found myself acknowledging other Blacks generally by nodding and not by speaking. Most of the people who boarded the train from 96th Street south seemed to be from a different cut of the cloth. Most, it seemed to me, wore blue or grey suits, often pin-striped, and would be reading either the New York Times or Wall Street Journal, not the New York Daily News or New York Post. I would laughingly think, *"This is New York City's version of Jim Crow."* Jim Crow was a racial caste system designed to keep Blacks at the bottom of society. Under Jim Crow etiquette, for example, in the southern states:

A black male could not offer his hand (to shake hands} with a white male because it implied being socially equal. Obviously, a black male could not offer his hand or any other part of his body to a white woman, because he risked being accused of rape (Jim Crow Museum).

Whites, who caught the train at stops south of 125th Street, would remain reticent, and so we followed suit. A recent Pew Research Center report, entitled *Race Is Central to Identity for Black Americans and Affects How They Connect with Each Other*, discusses this issue (Cox and Tamir 2022). What I understand now, but could not express growing up, is that America is a low-context, individualistic society, while Black Americans tend to behave in high-context, collectivist ways. Cultural context has a tremendous impact on the way we see ourselves and interact with each other. It influences one's behavior in terms of context, space, time, and information (Loewy, D. & Guffey, M. 2013)

> The United States has one of the most individualistic cultures in the world. Americans are more likely to prioritize themselves over a group and they value independence and autonomy (Rosenbaum 2018).

Black Americans are culturally high-context, collectivist individuals living in a low-context, individualistic society.

The US Army studied the impact of cultural context on civil affairs, which is when US armed forces engage with the civilian leadership of another country. The study's findings are presented in an article by the Association of The United States Army entitled, *Individualism versus Collectivism: Civil Affairs and the Clash of National Strategic Cultures*. The article mentions that China and Russia are both collectivist societies... Communist countries are collectivistic societies while the United States is an individualistic society. The article explains that this difference in cultural context is important because it helps one to better understand the behaviors and the decisions that leaders and country states make. *Could it be possible that Black Americans, from a cultural context perspective, align better with a collectivist society like Communist Vietnam?*

I grew up in Harlem on 137th Street between 7th Avenue (renamed Adam Clayton Powell Jr. Boulevard in 1974) and Lenox Avenue (renamed Malcolm X Boulevard in 1987). One of my mentors growing up, Mr. Dabney Montgomery, was my religious teacher at the AME Zion Methodist Church next door to the apartment building where I lived with my parents. He served with the distinguished Red Tails during World War II. *Wow,* I remember thinking as a kid, I know a *Tuskegee Airman.*

Many years after my return from Vietnam, I learned that Mr. Montgomery was born in Selma, Alabama and that he had

been very active in the fight for civil rights. He served as a bodyguard for Reverend Martin Luther King Jr. during the 1965 March from Selma to Montgomery, Alabama. After Mr. Montgomery's death in 2016 136th Street between Adam Clayton Powell Blvd and Frederick Douglass Blvd (8th Avenue) was given the name Dabney Montgomery Place. It was a real honor to know him, and it was perhaps his example that made it conceivable that I would someday proudly serve to protect our homeland against foreign and domestic enemies, and in particular, against the ideology of nondemocratic regimes, which was prevalent during my childhood years.

On 135th Street and then 7th Avenue, just around the corner and two blocks south from my block, was Small's Paradise, a nightclub and restaurant. While sit-ins and freedom rides were taking place throughout the southern states to fight segregation, Whites and Blacks came together to dance at Small's; it was regularly packed with educated and moneyed Blacks and Whites who came to hear the big bands play, and to see the floor shows. Just a block south of Small's was Count Basie's Bar, where you could find sport figures enjoying live jazz. Around the corner and a block north, at 138th Street and 7th Avenue, was the Red Rooster, a bar and restaurant where Black judges, lawyers, politicians, and other prominent people hung out. While Blacks were fighting for integrated education in the southern states, in New York City, one could choose to attend virtually any public high school within the five boroughs one wanted to attend. The top schools required passing an entry test, but you could get into those schools if you passed the test. I chose to go to the high school Big Ralph and Bill went to. It was a good academic school, DeWitt Clinton, an all-boys school in the Bronx. Among the graduates were many noteworthy individuals, including writer James Baldwin; Nobel Prize winner and physicist Robert Hofstadter; Pulitzer Prize winners Mel Powell, Henry, and Robert Butler; the first Black conductor of the New York Philharmonic, Dean Dixon; creator of the musical, *The Wiz*, Kenneth Harper; actor and civil rights activist Burt Lancaster (who turned down the lead role in the Vietnam War film, *Platoon*); fashion designer Ralph Lauren; US Congressman Charles Rangel; and the list goes on and on (*Wikipedia* 2022).

Just before graduating from high school in 1965, I received a brochure from Lynchburg College in Lynchburg, Virginia. I was not certain that the brochure was intended for me (being Black) but I seriously considered applying. What I didn't know at the time was that Lynchburg College was founded by a man who served in the Union Army and admired Abraham Lincoln for his anti-slavery stance. And about the time I got the brochure, many at Lynchburg was thinking about racial equality (Staff,

Open the doors 2017). In the end, I did not apply to the school because I had great difficulty getting pass "lynch" as part of the name of the college and its town.

In 1926, a Lynchburg College school leader encouraged the local YMCA to invite the Black scientist George Washington Carver from Tuskegee to speak there. When the College received a grant in the 1930s to study a societal issue, it chose to study problems of racial discrimination in the South. But when Black students from Virginia State College, a nearby Black teachers college came to participate in an educational program and began dancing with Lynchburg's White female students, the college's President was nearly fired over the issue. Newspaper headlines read, "Communist influences at work in Lynchburg College" (Staff, *Open the doors* 2017).

After high school, I was accepted to a summer program at New York University, where I learned computer programming. Upon completion of that program, I worked my way into a full-time computer programming job while I taught programming at night a couple days a week and simultaneously attended college a couple of nights. With all of that going on in my life, I was afraid of being drafted because I would lose or delay my momentum to succeed.

I would call home after work virtually every day to ask my mother what was in the mail for me. I was anxious about the draft because they were drafting guys my age who did not have a deferment. One could avoid being drafted, at least until the age of twenty-four, by going to college full-time and maintaining good grades; I did not. I did not go to college full-time, that is. You could avoid the draft by getting married; however, on August 26, 1965, the year I was graduated from high school, President Johnson signed Executive Order 11241, bringing the married man deferment to an end. You could be deferred from the draft if you worked in certain professions, such as a teacher or policeman. The teacher deferment worked for me because I was teaching computer programming, albeit part-time, but I didn't know at the time that it was the reason I was not called up to serve. Ironically, one could not go to school part-time and be deferred, but one could teach part-time and not be drafted. One had to be able to afford college to be deferred from the draft. When I could no longer handle the workload required of a full-time computer programmer, part-time teacher, and part-time student, I stopped teaching. I needed the full-time job to support myself, and I needed to go to school to cement my future. I saw teaching as something I enjoyed and was good at, but it was mostly to the benefit of my students, so I thought. I had no idea of the reality that it was part-time teaching that was keeping me out of harm's way. I quit teaching and was drafted in November 1969, at the age of twenty-two. Just a month later, on December 1, 1969, the selective service started a draft lottery, that is, a lottery which was used to determine the order by which one would be called for induction into the military. Had I quit teaching just thirty days later, just thirty days, I would have been put into the lottery and it would have been the luck of the draw.

The first drawing included men born between 1944 and 1950; I was born in 1947. Based upon my birth date, I would have had a lottery number of 163. Men with lottery numbers below 196 were drafted, and so even had I waited thirty days, 'Nam was my destiny. Being drafted meant I had to give up my job where I was being paid extremely well as a computer programmer, and I had to give up going to evening college. I was to become GI (Government Issue), to be trained in the art of war, and be given in return one-tenth of what I was being paid in civilian life. But I now had the opportunity to serve my country, as did Blacks who fought in America's wars before me. I was in the Army now.

IN THE ARMY NOW

I thought about my experience marching military-style with the Eastsiders Drum and Bugle Corps, which was the merger of two corps, the Cavaliers Drum & Bugle Corps from Harlem and the Eastsiders Drum & Bugle Corps from Manhattan's predominately Puerto Rican Lower Eastside neighborhood. Though not a military unit, we practiced our drill for competition on the drill floor of the 369th Armory on 141st Street and 5th Avenue, which was the home of the 369th Regiment, the Harlem Hellfighters. The 369th was also nicknamed the Black Rattlers; the French called them Men of Bronze, but it was the Germans who referred to them as the Hellfighters. The Hellfighters was the first African-American regiment to serve in Europe during World War I, well before my time, and they saw action in World War II, before my time. During WWI, the US military assigned them to fight with the French, requiring that they wear French uniforms because the White US Soldiers refused to serve with Blacks back then, but the 369th was in the fight to show their patriotism to the US, and they wanted to fight for democracy both in Europe and at home. For the men of the 369th, it had to be a perplexing time. No doubt, Hitler was a racist, for he wanted to rid the world of Jews, and he was certainly no fan of Blacks. He didn't even like jazz ... go figure! Within a year after their return to the States, the domestic fight was on. Race riots broke out in twenty-six cities (*Wikipedia* 2022).

During World War I, the 369th Marching Band, which had as many as one-third of its members from Puerto Rico, was considered one of the most famous military bands in Europe. It introduced jazz to the Europeans. Six days after Armistice Day, the band marched up 5th Avenue in New York, starting at 61st Street, and into Harlem and up Lenox Avenue. I could only imagine the excitement felt by the people of Harlem as the 369th Regiment marched by. Nothing got my heart pumping with eagerness to serve my country more than to imagine what it must have been like to see the 369th's homecoming as I watched the people on our sidelines march and dance to the beat of our drums as we came up 5th Avenue for Columbus Day, or up 7th Avenue in Harlem for the Afro-American Day parade.

The Eastsiders, as was the 369th Marching Band, comprised of Blacks and Puerto Ricans. All but a couple of the drummers were previously members of the Cavaliers, and the horn line (bugle players) was mostly Puerto Ricans from the former Eastsiders. However, my time with the Eastsiders was disrupted by the draft.

After my return home from 'Nam, I immediately rejoined the corps. It had become a senior drum and bugle corps. I found

my homecoming reality to be quite different from what members of the 369th experienced. There were no parades to celebrate Vietnam Veterans returning home from the War. In fact, Pete Seeger released his song, "Bring 'Em Home," in 1969 the very year I was drafted. We were viewed not as heroes, but as  outcasts because we had fought in the unpopular war, Vietnam, and we were even called "baby killers" by some.

Before being drafted, I found just entering the armory through its heavy, iron doors for drum corps practice, and speaking to men in uniform roaming the building, gave me a sense of pride and the proclivity to join the fight against Communist Vietnam. However, unlike the Blacks, particularly Southern Blacks who served in the military prior to Vietnam, I did not necessarily view my service as an opportunity to show my patriotism because the Vietnam War was very controversial. Nor did I necessarily see it as a way to earn my place as an equal citizen of the US. Though the 1964 Civil Rights Act offered a glimmer of hope, many before me had served and saw no return on their investment. I had ambivalent feelings about the Vietnam War and would hear the anti-Vietnam War perspective being preached just around the corner from where I lived.

On 138th Street, US Congressman and pastor of the Abyssinian Baptist Church, Adam Clayton Powell Jr., was vehemently opposed to the Vietnam War. He felt that the US was imposing a democracy on the folks of Southeast Asia when the free and equal rights of many of our own citizens here at home were being denied. He was a national figure, an Afro-American politician whose perspective undoubtedly took into account his broad and deep understanding of national affairs. He was someone whose opinion mattered to me, and he was able to broaden my own parochial view of the issues of the day. I was holding on to the perspective that what was important at the time were issues that had a local community or personal dimension to them. From my very provincial viewpoint, Jim Crow and racism were Southern problems. In fact, I had difficulty understanding why a Black person would choose to live in the South, given what was taking place there. Why not move North or even West? Why not join in on the Great Migration?

I thought about other noteworthy individuals who I was told were former congregants of my church, Mother AME Zion ...

in the North … in Harlem. There was Paul, Fred, Sojourner, and Harriet. I grew up with Paul's nephew Gregory Smith, and Paul's brother Benjamin Robeson, who was pastor of Mother Zion when I attended. Paul Robeson was said to be a Communist. He fought for change in that he sought equality and fair treatment for all Americans. His unwillingness to conform socially caused him great difficulty. And Paul's role in the play, *All God's Chillun Got Wings*, brought threats from the KKK because in the play a White woman was to kiss his hand (Ellis 2003). Fred, that is, Frederick Douglass, was an abolitionist who escaped slavery. He taught himself how to read, and he traveled as far as England to speak against slavery. Sojourner Truth, who was born into slavery, fostered change as an impressive speaker, preacher, activist, and abolitionist. And born into slavery, Harriet Tubman was known for being the conductor of the Underground Railroad that led many slaves North to freedom. Though I never had the pleasure of meeting any of them, their lives and the lives of congregants who came before them set a tone, a tenor, that could be felt in 1796 the day the church was founded, and even as I attended.

I was now beginning to worry about being drafted. I could not learn and think about Black history and not acknowledge that there was a fight at home, on the Western front, to be fought for the civil rights of all Americans. For me, it would have been certainly more comprehensible if I were to be drafted and ordered to serve as a soldier in a fight for civil rights in the South, not of Vietnam, but of the United States.

I came to believe that ideologies espoused during and as a result of WWII by the Fascists (Germany and Italy) and the Communists (Russia, North Vietnam, and China) would limit, if given the chance to persist, our individual rights; and I concluded that, since Mr. Montgomery served in the military during that time, he would be the person whose opinion I would take under advisement. However, two decades had passed since WWII, and

I questioned if it would be wiser to follow my father's tutelage. I had to decide. Should I follow the lead of my childhood mentor who served proudly in the military, albeit in WWII, or take the advice of my father who, like many of my contemporaries, had no appetite to serve? I was further conflicted because I did not have a good foundation from which to make such an important personal decision. I was not a student of history, and I shied away from reading about current events in favor of studying math, business, and technology.

Big Ralph was small in stature. He was about five feet six inches tall, and weighed maybe 145 pounds in wet clothes. He was a naturalized citizen from Trinidad, an immigrant, who had not served in anyone's military. He used metaphors and allegories when he spoke, making it at times tough to understand what he really meant, but when it came to the war in Vietnam, his stance was crystal. Fighting in Vietnam, from Big Ralph's perspective, was "for the birds."

I believe young men my age looked at the war in Vietnam from one of several perspectives. There were those who did not hesitate to enlist in one of the branches of the service, for they wanted to join in the fight. Some came from families with long lineages of military men, with many actually being able to trace their family's sacraments as far back as the Civil War. These men saw themselves as not merely following a family tradition but as patriots defending their country and its way of life against Communism. Other contemporaries joined the service because they were told and convinced that "the military will make a man out of you." Then there were those who simply wanted to escape what troubled them at home, and what better way to run from their problems than to join the military and be seen as patriotic and brave?

The Harlem race riot, which took place the summer after my high school junior year, was precipitated by an off-duty police officer shooting and killing a Black teenager. It was so upsetting that it gave me pause with regards to serving in the military and possibly having to go to Vietnam. And following the assassination of Martin Luther King Jr. in 1968, there were riots in more than 110 U.S. cities (*Encyclopedia of U.S. history*, 2023). I thought about the young men who were able to get into the National Guard, and how they were being used to stave off riots here at home, riots in Detroit and in Chicago, and many other urban areas that were fruitful for the draft, even as the people in those areas were being denied their civil rights.

Speaking out along the streets of Harlem, often on 125th Street and Lenox Avenue, was Malcolm X, who urged Afro-Americans to take a more aggressive stance than the nonviolent approach, which was Reverend Martin Luther King Jr.'s approach toward gaining civil rights. I graduated from high school in 1965, the year that Malcolm X was assassinated. The assassination took place, not in the South, but in the Audubon Ballroom, a dance hall in Harlem—a place my family visited often and knew well.

In a 1967 sermon, at the Riverside Church in Harlem Rev, Dr. King Jr. addressed the question that I wanted desperately to find an answer to, "Why am I opposed to the war in Vietnam?" It was powerful. And about the same time were also tormenting words coming from Congressman Adam Clayton Powell Jr., which gave me much food for thought. He asked rhetorically, "Why should Blacks, particularly Southern Blacks, go all the way to Southeast Asia to fight in a war for Vietnam's democracy when there was a battle right here at home to be fought?" And by the time I was graduated in 1965, war was in the air like a dark cloud hanging overhead; there were definite signs of inclement times ahead. Three years later Reverend Martin Luther King Jr. was assassinated, this time in the South.

Most young men my age did not enlist and did not avoid the draft by running to Canada, but rather sought ways to dodge the draft without being classified as a draft dodger. They would achieve this by going to college, by getting married, or by getting a job that would give them a deferment. Full-time college students were given a deferment for as long as they remained in school in good standing. Before Vietnam, a college student would typically take four years to graduate. Now it was not uncommon for a student to take six years to graduate. I wonder if there is a connection? Al Franken notes:

> During Vietnam, I was in college, enjoying my student deferment. The government wisely felt that, in my case, military service was less important than completing my studies to prepare me for my chosen career: comedian (www.brainyquote.com/topics/ military service).

Teachers, policemen, correction officers, and a few other professionals, not comedians, were given deferments. Also, one could join the National Guard or a military reserve unit, and thereby greatly reduce the chances of being sent to Vietnam. For those individuals who were firmly against the war and what it stood for, going to Canada was still a most plausible option, for if you did not run to Canada and you made it known that you were a conscientious objector, you could be drafted and sent to Vietnam as a medic with no weapon, and a red cross on your helmet, a bull's-eye.

I was confused as to what I should do. Deep down, I wanted to evade the draft. But if I did, others would see me as a traitor, or worse yet, a coward. And it mattered to me greatly what others thought of me, even today as I think back. If Uncle Sam, through my local draft board, "invited" me to serve, I recalled thinking, it would be in my best interest to go and not to run off to Canada as a few did, because not to report as ordered would make me a draft dodger, which would ultimately, I thought, taint me for the rest of my life. Finally, I would do what all patriotic American boys of my ilk did … I waited to be invited by the President of the United States to put my life on the line in America's fight against Communism.

Then came the 1968 Tet Offensive when the VC and North Vietnamese Army made a major assault on South Vietnam. I was drafted a year later and sent to Fort Jackson in Columbia, South Carolina, for basic training, and then to Fort Gordon in Augusta, Georgia, for radio teletype and leadership schools. I felt almost as uncomfortable being in the South of the United States as I did in being in the queue for Vietnam. And now I was in the midst of fighting a two-front war. In military terms, a two-front war is one in which fighting occurs in different geographic locations at the same time. Accordingly, it is virtually impossible for a soldier to be sent to fight on more than one front, unless he is Afro-American.

As a Black soldier, I was fighting on two fronts simultaneously. On the Eastern front was the in-country war against the Democratic Republic of Vietnam (North Vietnamese) and Vietcong. They were fighting for the reunification and independence of their country, and even as we were adversaries, the North Vietnamese and Afro-Americans during 'Nam were "comrades" in an ideological battle against US oppression. Ironically, Afro-American Soldiers were ordered to fight alongside steadfast Soldiers of the Confederate States of America who continued the Lost Cause ideology, which "emerged in the decades after the war among former Confederate generals and politicians" ("Lost Cause of the Confederacy" 2019). The Lost Cause ideology states that the Civil War was just and heroic. In the 1950s and 1960s, Confederate monuments were built, and textbooks were written explaining the "true" reasons for the Civil War, supporting white supremacy and Jim Crow Laws. Thus, on the Western front was the continuing battle for civil rights both in-country and at home. And all was anything but quiet on the Western front.

After the Army's basic training, advanced individual training (AIT), and leadership schools, I had a strong, positive feeling about the men with whom I trained and would serve, and of my country. I had been completely indoctrinated. By the completion of basic combat training, my morale was really high and I had esprit de corps. After basic, I went to ROC (Radio Operator Course) for AIT, where I learned the skills and responsibilities of a radioman and radio teletype operator (05C20). It was at the ROC that I learned that the military no longer used the terms *able* and *baker* in its phonetic alphabet, as in the WWII movies I'd watched,  but rather *alpha* and *bravo*. I began to wonder what else was different about the military today versus the WWII military. I learned that v was phonetically Victor, and c was Charlie, but use of the phonetics *Victor Charlie* when referring to the VC was frowned upon ... we did not want to speak of Charlie as a victor; I used just Charlie.

After AIT, I was sent to leadership school and was trained to carry out the duties of radio teletype team chief. In less than six months, I was a proud buck sergeant, E-5. Guys like me were often referred to as "shake and bakes" because of the rapid rate at which we were promoted to fill leadership shortages in the critical 05C MOS (military occupational specialty). The term "shake and bake" came from a breadcrumb product developed in 1965 by General Foods. You would place raw chicken or pork in a bag of flavored breadcrumbs, shake the bag until the crumbs stuck to the meat, then microwaved or baked the meat for a few minutes, and voilà ... it was ready to be served. We were shake and bakes, ready to serve as NCOs in the US Army in Vietnam.

At the height of the Vietnam War, up-and-coming commo guys who wanted to learn the art of radio operation would walk into a classroom and see a huge number five written on the chalkboard.

Inevitably, someone's curiosity would win out and they'd ask what the big number meant. The instructor would then calmly tell them, "That's your life expectancy, in seconds, in a firefight. So, listen up and you might learn something that'll keep you alive Milzarski, 2021).

IN-COUNTRY

I n-country, American Soldiers, Marines, and Sailors of all backgrounds fought together for a common cause, one that most could not articulate other than to say, "We must deny Ho Chi Minh's Vietnamese the opportunity to spread Communism." The US military was programmed to fight as a team; and yet, it was not uncommon for one to see a Confederate flag, or a Southern state flag that approximated the Confederate flag, flying on top of a bunker. The Confederate battle flag was inspiration for the Georgia and Mississippi state flags. They blatantly bore a most recognizable symbol of the Confederacy. These flags were a stark reminder that approximately one hundred years prior to 'Nam, eleven Southern states seceded from the Union to form their own country, the Confederate States of America, which wanted to continue African slavery. Symbols of the Confederacy were now on display in Vietnam, antagonizing Black Soldiers.

Often, Black Soldiers displayed pictures of civil rights activist and events from the civil rights movement in their bunkers. You might find Martin Luther King Jr., Malcolm X, Angela Davis, Andrew Young, or Rosa Parks over their bunks, not in response to the displays of the Confederate and Southern state flags, but in support of the civil rights movement. However, Rockwell's depiction of Ruby Bridges, the young Black girl who was escorted by US marshals into an all-White school in New Orleans in 1960, seemed particularly troubling to many of the White Soldiers, perhaps because it was a reminder that segregation had come to an end. One federal marshal described Ruby Bridges, saying, "She showed a lot of courage ... She just marched along like a little soldier."

By the time most of us got in-country, the Jim Crow laws had become virtually defunct from the passing of the Civil Rights Act in 1964 and the Voting Rights Act in 1965. Even so, the Vietnamese radio personality Trinh Thi Ngo, known to GIs as Hanoi Hannah, habitually reminded Black Soldiers that we were victims of bigotry, and she seemed to realize—even when it was not clear to us—that it would take much more than revisions in America's laws to dissipate the dark cloud of racism which hung over our country. Hanoi Hannah attempted to contribute to Hanoi's war effort by daily broadcasting divisive messages along racial lines, demoralizing Black Soldiers, and encouraging Blacks to lay down their arms. Her messages were not effective in helping the Hanoi war effort, but it did help keep the civil rights movement alive in the bunkers.

Soon, I found myself having to work outside of my MOS and above my pay grade as the men in my unit, who had come to 'Nam before me, awoke on their last day and rotated home. The 'Nam tour of duty was twelve months, often expressed by Soldiers as "365 days and a wake-up." I became, by default, the section leader for the 20th Combat Engineer Battalion's Headquarters Company's Communication Section. The section consisted of about eight men from various states and Puerto Rico. Unfortunately for me, one of the draftees who came into the section as a replacement was a Southerner from Georgia.

Edward seemed not to have gotten the message that the Civil War was over; that it had been over for more than a hundred years. And that the North had won! But he was from Albany,

Georgia. Albany was such a racist city that Martin Luther King Jr., after demonstrating there on three separate occasions and being arrested each time, agreed to no longer demonstrate there (Albany Movement 2018). It is not surprising, therefore, that Edward would have a problem with a Black man, me, being in charge and able to put at risk the lives of White men, like him.

Our communications section needed to be in constant communications with the 4th Infantry Division, which was on the other side of Dragon Mountain. Unfortunately, mountains block FM radio waves making FM communication virtually impossible, and we found our AM radio to be unreliable particularly in bad weather. Consequently, we kept a relay station on top of Dragon Mountain and stationed two to three Soldiers there to ensure its continued operation. Edward, saw it completely  incomprehensible that a Black sergeant could order White Soldiers to perform such a risky assignment. His influence on the men with whom I was "serving time" was so negative that I found myself having to work very hard at developing and keeping good working relationships with the men in the section, while at the same time doing all I could to win over Edward's respect for me as his leader. To further complicate the situation, a few of the Black combat engineers resented me for spending so much time with White Soldiers, to which I insisted, "You want me to be able to work with them and to lead them! When the shit hits the fan," I reminded them, "those are the men you must depend upon to call in aviation gunships and medical evacuation choppers such as *Headhunter and Undertaker.*"

During the day, the US military effectively controlled the South Vietnam Central Highlands region, referred to as II Corps, which was headquartered in Pleiku … but nights were a different story. You see, at night, our daytime enemy "Charlie" morphed into "Mr. Charles," someone worthy of great respect because he—or she, for that matter (unlike the US military at that time, the Vietcong fought with a gender-integrated force)—controlled the turf outside of our base camp. They even had maps detailing what was inside of our camp, which they could use to guide sapper attacks and to direct mortar fire on us. The information for the maps were provided by the Vietnamese people, the few we mistakenly trusted and employed during the day to clean the mess hall, to work as hooch girls, or to serve in various other capacities in base camp. It was virtually impossible to know who was with us or who was against us.

I always felt safe around the Montagnard people. They were strong allies and were known to be fierce fighters. In the end, however, their alliance to the United States cost them dearly. Some estimate that over 50 percent of the adult Montagnard males were killed during 'Nam, and after the war, many of their women were sterilized by the Vietnamese government (*Vietnam's blueprint for ethnic cleansing - europarl.europa.eu*).

In August 1971, the battalion was ordered back to the States, to Fort Campbell, Kentucky. I was among the few men in headquarters company, 20th Combat Engineers, who was not sent home with the battalion but was instead reassigned and attached to an ARVN unit at Weight-Davis, a rock quarry and fire support base some forty kilometers south of Pleiku. I recall one evening, before leaving for Weight-Davis, sitting around in the hooch and listening to the guys in my section who would be going home, describe in great detail what they planned to do when they got back to "the world." I found myself staring at Edward, whose complexion seemed more pale than usual and who appeared to be looking right through me with a blank stare. I had seen that look before, not just in 'Nam, but as a young person growing up. It was the look and stare of death. Was what I saw in Edward a premonition, or was it from some deep-seated unconscious anger I felt toward him because I saw him as a recovering racist and xenophobe who was on his way back home like an alcoholic headed back to the bar. Now that we were close, I'm sure, if he continued to think of me as a Black man, he was telling himself that I was not like the others. Yet, I did not want to think I was subconsciously wishing he would not make it home. Over the months we served together he became someone I could count on; he knew he could count on me, and he seem to respect me as a leader.

As the battalion began readying to go home, I (along with four other men) was ordered to pack and head for Weight-Davis. A few days after our arrival there, we received a radio transmission from the guys we'd left behind at base camp communications, letting us know that Edward had loaded in to a 3/4-ton truck, additional equipment he felt was essential for our assignment, and he was headed for our location.

He arrived safely at Weight-Davis late that evening. We quickly unloaded the truck, and we begged Edward to stay the night. "Remember, Mr. Charles will be watching," we told him. Edward wanted to return to Pleiku before it was noticed that he was gone and what he had done. Besides, the battalion was to pull out soon, and he did not want to miss the big bird back to "the world." We stayed in constant radio contact with Edward as he headed back, as did the communication guys at the other end in Pleiku. Then we lost contact with him as did Pleiku communications.

It tormented me not to know what ultimately happened to Edward. Did he make it home? When I got home, I wanted to contact his family to find out if he made it, but knowing his background I didn't think his family would be open to hearing from me. Then after many agonizing years, my son Richard Victor suggested that we go to the Vietnam Veterans Memorial in Washington D.C. ... Edward's name was on The Wall.

BACK IN THE WORLD

Growing up, my parents did not speak about racism much, if at all, with my brother and me. I believe they didn't want to put a racism cloud over our heads. They wanted us to believe, without reservation, that we were as good as anyone else; however, given Nita's visible outrage in certain situations, we knew racism existed. It was her stance against racism that helped us to feel worthy. I remember how angry she would get when we were obviously being followed in a retail store by security, or when she was shown a red dress by a salesperson. She felt that White people thought Black people much preferred anything red, and that we favored eating chicken and watermelon. Even today, I find myself having difficulty eating watermelon and fried chicken in public because of these stereotypes, though quietly I acknowledge truly enjoying watermelon and fried chicken at home. Perhaps I must take the advice of Shirley Chisholm who said:

> We must reject not only the stereotypes that others have of us but also those that we have of ourselves (Winslow 2018).

In his book, *Citizen Soldiers*, Stephen Ambrose said that during World War II, when German Soldiers were captured and brought to the States, they were treated better than America's

Black Soldiers. In one of Ambrose's anecdotes, a group of Black Soldiers traveling through a Southern state during the war was poorly treated because of Jim Crow Laws. They were told to go to the back door of a restaurant to be served a sandwich and coffee, even as German POWs were seated indoors to be served. And after President Truman signed Executive Order 9981 addressing civil rights issues in the military, Black Soldiers still had to go to the back door of restaurants at many nonmilitary public places.

I thought about the trip I took by chartered bus as a Boy Scout to the Philmont Scout Ranch and how we actually got to meet with President Truman when we visited the Truman Library in Missouri. The one and only question I could think to ask him was, "How do you feel about being a past president?" He replied (I paraphrase), "I am a former president, I've not passed." I was not sure whether he was saying that light heartedly or if I was being criticized? I thought back to what my ninth-grade teacher told me: "There are no two words in the English language that mean exactly the same thing." I was so uninformed back then about the English language, and about the civil rights struggle (and sex) that I was not certain if I properly acknowledged or perhaps insulted the man who, by signing Executive Order 9981, made it possible for me to be able to stay with other White scouts at government military facilities and government-managed lands without concern for the racist Jim Crow Laws as we traveled into the South. Executive Order 9981, signed in 1948, meant the end of segregation and racism in the armed forces ... sort of.

As we entered the mid-1960s, opposition to the Vietnam War intensified. It continued to intensify overtime until 1973 when the draft and combat operations in Vietnam were suspended. In 1972, about a year after I returned from 'Nam, actress and anti-war activist Jane Fonda, dubbed Hanoi Jane, was caught fraternizing with the North Vietnamese Army. She went as far as to be photographed sitting at a North Vietnamese antiaircraft gun. It was the type of weapon used to shoot down US planes, US planes like the one flown by Captain John McCain. Let me underscore that Jane Fonda, during the war, sat in an enemy antiaircraft gun while fraternizing with enemy Soldiers. And though many of the men and women who had served in 'Nam may have seen the war as improper and wanted it to come to an end, you would hear them say, "I am not fond of Jane Fonda." Jane Fonda did ultimately apologize saying, "It hurts me and it will to my grave that I made a huge, huge mistake that made a lot of people think I was against the Soldiers (*Jane Fonda: Hanoi Jane Photo was a 'huge mistake'* 2015)." To be fair, Jane Fonda stood against the Vietnam War, but not the US military in 'Nam, and she stood for equality and against racism at home. Her platform paralleled that of Dr. Rev. Martin Luther King, Jr.

Activists against the war and for civil rights were of all races and professions. Comedian Dick Gregory was arrested several times fighting for civil rights and for protesting the Vietnam War. Often, he used satirical humor to make a point one of which remains with me:

> Last time I was down South I walked into this restaurant, and this white waitress came up to me and said: "We don't serve colored people here." I said: "that's all right, I don't eat colored people. Bring me a whole fried chicken (Dick Gregory)."

Ho Chi Minh started out as a nationalist revolutionary who led Vietnam's rebellion against French colonialism. The French was to a great extend funded by the United States, and thus, Ho Chi Minh saw Americans as being hypocritical. America started out as a colony, gained its independence through revolution, but then participated in the colonization of Vietnam. The US was endeavoring to prohibit Vietnam's independence. Uncle Ho (Ho Chi Minh) is quoted as saying:

> I think I know the American people and I don't understand how they can support their involvement in this war (Vietnam). Is the Statue of Liberty standing on her head? (Whitman 1969).

I believe the Statue of Liberty was standing on her head when Jewish refugees were denied entry into the United States during World War II. And she knows how the Montagnards who fought with the US in 'Nam got totally screwed once we left. She was watching as Afghans who fought with the US during the Afghan War were being denied entry to the US, and many never even got to the border.

Blacks who fought in the two Great World Wars came home expecting to be welcomed and appreciated, but rather were mistreated, and in some cases, their homes were torched, and some men were lynched. "It is well-known that the Black race is the most oppressed and the most exploited of the human family...," noted Ho Chi Minh, and he said, "American Negroes still endure atrocious moral and material sufferings, of which the most cruel and horrible is the custom of lynching."

Many years following the War, the US's relationship with Communist Vietnam improved greatly, as evidenced by the fact that the US has been importing billions of dollars of goods from the Communist Socialist Republic of Vietnam ... much more than it has been exporting to the Communist country. If poor, unskilled US laborers had difficulty finding work before 'Nam, after 'Nam, it became even more difficult as America exported jobs to Vietnam more than goods. As a result, US companies increased their profits by employing cheap Communist labor, thereby dropping their labor costs at the expense of US workers in the States. We have become a global society, for better or for worse, with all of the trappings, good or bad, that come with globalization.

In 2008, the US elected Barack Obama its first Black president raising hopes that race relations in the US would finally improve. And there was the expectation that the US would get better at handling international affairs with President Obama at the helm.

> In 2009, shortly after Obama took office, residents in many countries expressed a sharp increase in confidence in the ability of the U.S. president to do the right thing in international affairs (Dimock 2017).

Yet, I wondered how long it would take before we would see President Obama treated as a Black man, not as the president of the United States. I wondered when America's relationship with Blacks would once again head south, because there were a number of wealthy and politically connected people who did not like having a Black president.

> There was a time not so long ago when Americans, regardless of their political stripes, rallied 'round their president. Once elected, the man who won the White House was no longer viewed as a Republican or Democrat, but the president of the United States ...

> Suddenly President Barack Obama, with the potential to become an exceptional president, has become the glaring exception to that unwritten, patriotic rule (Thomas 2014).

Unlike the Germans, the Japanese, and the Vietnamese, whose relationships with America got increasingly better after warring with the US, American Blacks who fought bravely for America in every war from and since the Revolutionary War, continue to remain in a societal cesspool.

NYU Associate Professor Hannah Gurman, writing in the *Washington Post*, made this point with respect to Vietnam: "...as with the Civil War, racism was deeply embedded in the [Vietnam] conflict (Gurman, 2021)." And according to her, President Nixon expressed his belief that nobody would care if "these little brown people [Montagnards] were slaughtered and castrated by North Vietnamese forces." And when the White Southern Soldiers returned home, Professor Gurman notes:

> Nixon was quick to appeal to them by simultaneously denouncing antiwar activists and propping up Southern white pride with the dog-whistle rhetoric of law and order and states' rights (Gurman, 2021).

As time for a soldier to return home to the states neared, it was a common practice for a short-timer to send home a letter warning their loved ones that they were coming, and what to expect from their behavior. The typical letter would read, in part, something like this (author unknown):

> Dear Family and Friends,

> ... show no alarm if (name of returning soldier) insists on carrying a weapon to the dinner table, looks around for his steel pot when offered a chair, or wakes you up in the middle of the night for guard duty. Keep cool when he pours gravy on his dessert at dinner or mixes peaches with his Seagram's VO. Pretend not to notice if he acts dazed, eats with his fingers instead of silverware and prefers C-rations to steak. Take it with a smile when he insists on digging up the garden to fill sandbags for the bunker he is building. Be tolerant when he takes his blanket and sheet off the bed and puts them on the floor to sleep on for (name of returning soldier) is coming home.

"What pig did not flush the toilet?" someone blurted out at my welcome home celebration. Embarrassingly, I begged for forgiveness, explaining that I had gone more than a year without having to flush a toilet. Jackie tells how, when her brother returned from 'Nam that he would always promise to take a very short shower because he was concerned that he would use more than his share of water. And virtually all of us came home lacking the pride in country and the self-respect that we had taken to 'Nam because of the guilt and shame that was spat upon us. My biggest lost was in recognizing myself, in recognizing who I had been before I'd served my country honorably.

As the 25th Anniversary of the end of the Vietnam War approached, Senator McCain went to Hanoi in an effort to strengthen US trade ties with Vietnam. However, his recollection of his stay at the Hanoi Hilton apparently detracted from this mission Mydans, 2000). "The wrong guys," won the war he would say. And referring to the five years he spent at the Hanoi Hilton he remembered the prison guards noting, "I still bear them ill will, not because of what they did to me, but because of what they did to some of my friends - including killing some of them." And yet, he was able to find something positive to share with his wife Cindy and 13-year-old son Jack. They got a traditional Vietnamese tonic - rice liquor with a snake in the bottle (Mydans, 2000). If that's Vietnamese food culture, I pass.

Fourteen years after I returned home from Vietnam, New York City had what was said to be at the time the biggest parade in the city (United Press International 1985). It was for Vietnam Vets. I took a break from my work at Salomon Brothers, at 55 Water Street, to walk over to Broadway to get a glimpse of the parade. I watched as fellow Vietnam Vets crossed the Brooklyn Bridge, and then down Broadway. I felt improperly attired, dressed in a business suit. Most of the bystanders had on something to identify themselves as a Vietnam Vet: a jungle hat, an Army jacket, medals on their chest. It was the first time since coming home from 'Nam in 1971 that I felt out of place because I was not wearing something to indicate that I was a Vietnam Veteran. It was the first time since getting home that, en masse, the citizens of New York visibly expressed their appreciation to us.

The parade down Broadway was a validation of our service. I was not to see such pride again until I went to Hanoi and saw Vets of the American war proudly display their ribbons on their uniforms as they paraded into the Ho Chi Minh Mausoleum. I started to feel a strong sense of connectedness with the Veterans of Hanoi who had fought in the American War, as I did with my fellow Veterans in New York City who had fought in the Vietnam War.

BIBLIOGRAPHY

Alberto Quintavalla & Klaus Heine (2019) Priorities and human rights, The International Journal of Human Rights, 23:4, 679-697, DOI: 10.1080/13642987.2018.1562917

ACLU history: The tragedy of the scottsboro boys (2010) American Civil Liberties Union. *Available at: https://www.aclu.org/other/aclu-history-tragedy-scottsboro-boys#:~:text=Their%20trials%20began%2012%20 days,death%20in%20the%20electric%20chair. (Accessed: January 14, 2023).*

Albany Movement (2018) The Martin Luther King, Jr., Research and Education Institute. Available at: https://kinginstitute.stanford.edu/encyclopedia/albany-movement (Accessed: January 16, 2023).

Altitude Life Hacks. "Average Height of Fortune 500 CEOS: 6'2." Last modified 2017. Accessed November 23, 2019. https://www.altitudelifehacks.com/blogs/altitudeshoes/average-height-of-fortune-500-ceos-62.

American Academy of Arts & Sciences. *The State of Languages in the US: A Statistical Portrait.* Month xxxx. Accessed September 5, 2022. https://www.amacad.org/sites/default/files/academy/multimedia/pdfs/publications/researchpapersmonographs/State-of-Languages-in-US.pdf.

American minority groups in the Vietnam War: A resource guide: Research Guides at Library of Congress. (n.d.). Retrieved January 29, 2023, from https://guides.loc.gov/american-minority-groups-in-the-vietnam-war#:~:text=Approximately%20300%2C000%20African%20Americans%20served,the%20U.S.%20Army's%20fatal%20casualties.

Andrews, E. (2017) The green book: The black travelers' guide to jim crow rerica, History.com. A&E Television Networks. Available at: https://www.history.com/news/the-green-book-the-black-travelers-guide-to-jim-crow-america (Accessed: January 14, 2023).

Apel, Therese. "Professor Tells Story of Ole Miss' First Black Student, Harry S. Murphy." *The Clarion-Ledger*, June 10, 2014. Accessed October 13, 2019. https://www.clarionledger.com/story/news/2014/06/10/professor-tells-story-ole-miss-first-black-student-harry-s-murphy/10281413/.

Association of the United States Army. *Individualism versus Collectivism: Civil Affairs and the Clash of National Strategic Cultures.* March 17, 2022. Accessed September 24, 2022. https://www.ausa.org/publications/individualism-versus-collectivism-civil-affairs-and-clash-national-strategic-cultures.

Baldwin, James. *The Fire Next Time.* New York: Dial Press, 1963.

Bell, C. "Racism: A Mental Illness?" Last modified 2004. Accessed January 3, 2020. https://ps.psychiatryonline.org/gun-violence/doi/pdfplus/10.1176/appi.ps.55.12.134.

BlackPast. "Adam Clayton Powell Sr. (1865–1953)" February 6, 2008. https://blackpast.org/aah/powell-sr-adam-clayton-1865-1953.

Burnett, Bob. "If You're Black, Get Back." *HuffPost* (blog). May 22, 2006. Updated May 25, 2011. Accessed September 17, 2022. https://www.huffpost.com/entry/if-youre-black-get-back_b_21426.

Centers for Disease Control and Prevention. "The Syphilis Study at Tuskegee Timeline." Accessed September 4, 2022. https://www.cdc.gov/tuskegee/timeline.htm.

Central Park five: The true story behind when they see us *(2019)* BBC News. *BBC. Available at: https://www.bbc.com/ news/newsbeat-48609693 (Accessed: January 15, 2023).*

Cervantes-Anguas, M. (2021). *The Limits Of Multiculturalism: Eurocentric Beauty Aesthetics And Colorism In Multicultural Advertising* (dissertation). California State University., Long Branch, CA.

Channing, C. *Just Lucky I Guess.* New York: Simon & Schuster, 2002.

Childs, David. "A Democratic Republic: What Is That???" *Democracy & Me* (blog). December 10, 2018. Accessed September 16, 2022. https://www.democracyandme. org/a-democratic-republic-what-is-that/.

Civil Rights. Community. movement. 2020) American Civil Liberties Union. Available at: https://www.aclu.org/other/civil-rights-community-movement (Accessed: January 15, 2023).

Cox, Kiana, and Tamir, Christine. *Race Is Central to Identity for Black Americans and Affects How They Connect with Each Other.* (Pew Research Center, April 14, 2022.) Accessed September 25, 2022. https://www.pewresearch.org/race-ethnicity/2022/04/14/race-is-central-to-identity-for-black-americans-and-affects-how-they-connect-with-each-other/.

Densu, K. (2023) ." Gale library of daily life: Slavery in america.. encyclopedia.com. 20 Dec. 2022, Encyclopedia.com. Encyclopedia.com. Available at: https://www.encyclopedia. com/humanities/applied-and-social-sciences-magazines/ house-slaves-overview (Accessed: January 14, 2023).

Dimock, Michael. *How America Changed during Barack Obama's Presidency.* (Pew Research Center.) January 10, 2017. Accessed September 25, 2022. https://www.pewresearch. org/2017/01/10/how-america-changed-during-barack- obamas-presidency/.

Ellis, Samantha "Paul Robeson in Othello, Savoy Theatre, 1930." *The Guardian,* September 3, 2003. Accessed September 25, 2022. https://www.theguardian.com/stage/2003/ sep/03/theatre.

Encyclopedia of U.S. history. encyclopedia.com. 14 Feb. 2023. (2023) Encyclopedia.com. Encyclopedia.com. Available at: https://www.encyclopedia.com/history/encyclopedias- almanacs-transcripts-and-maps/race-riots-1960s (Accessed: February 21, 2023).

Flanagan, C. (2018, October 22). Elizabeth Warren Has Lost Her Way. The Atlantic. Retrieved January 15, 2022, from https://www.theatlantic.com/ideas/archive/2018/10/ elizabeth-warren-shouldnt-have-shared-dna-test/573577/

Gandhi, Lakshmi. "How Two Vietnamese Sisters Led a Revolt against Chinese Invaders—in the 1st Century." *HISTORY.* Accessed October 5, 2022. https://www.history.com/news/ trung-sisters-vietnam-rebellion-han-dynasty.

Gelder, L.V. (1996) Medallion limits stem from the 30's, The New York Times. The New York Times. Available at: https:// www.nytimes.com/1996/05/11/nyregion/medallion-limits- stem-from-the-30-s.html (Accessed: January 13, 2023).

Griffin, John Howard. *Black Like Me*. New York, NY: Signet Books, 1962

Gurman, H. (2021) Perspective | as we rethink the Vietnam War, we have to grapple with its racial implications, The Washington Post. *WP Company. Available at: https://www. washingtonpost.com/news/made-by-history/wp/2017/10/06/ as-we-rethink-the-vietnam-war-we-have-to-grapple-with-its-racial-implications/ (Accessed: January 16, 2023).*

Haiphong, D. (2022) Malcolm X and Ho Chi Minh remind us of the roots of white supremacy in the aftermath of the Buffalo shooting, *Hampton Institute. Hampton Institute. Available at: https://www.hamptonthink.org/read/malcolm-x-and-ho-chi-minh-remind-us-of-the-roots-of-white-supremacy-in-the-aftermath-of-the-buffalo-shooting (Accessed: January 16, 2023).*

History. "Rosa Parks." Last modified January 19, 2022. Accessed January 23, 2023 https://www.history.com/ topics/black-history/rosa-parks.

History 101. "Trung Sisters: The Incredible Story of Vietnam's Rebel Leaders." Accessed October 5, 2022. https://www. history101.com/trung-sisters-vietnamese-rebel-leaders/.

History.com Editors (2009) *Rosa Parks, History.com*. A&E Television Networks. Available at: https://www.history. com/topics/black-history/rosa-parks (Accessed: January 7, 2023).

History.com Editors (2010a) Freedom riders, History.com. A&E Television Networks. Available at: https://www. history.com/topics/black-history/freedom-rides (Accessed: January 7, 2023).

History.com Editors (2010b) The Great Migration, History. com. A&E Television Networks. Available at: https://www. history.com/topics/black-history/great-migration (Accessed: January 13, 2023).

History.com Editors (2020) Vietnam declares its independence from France, History.com. A&E Television Networks. Available at: https://www.history.com/this-day-in-history/vietnam-independence-proclaimed (Accessed: August 27, 2023).

HUSL Library: A brief history of civil rights in the United States: Introduction (2023) Introduction - A Brief History of Civil Rights in the United States - HUSL Library at Howard University School of Law. Howard University, School of Law. Available at: https://library.law.howard.edu/civilrightshistory (Accessed: January 13, 2023).

Irish Americans And Whiteness (2023) Encyclopedia.com. Encyclopedia.com. Available at: https://www.encyclopedia. com/social-sciences/encyclopedias-almanacs-transcripts-and-maps/irish-americans-and-whiteness (Accessed: January 17, 2023).

Jane Fonda: Hanoi Jane Photo was a 'huge mistake' (2015) The Guardian. Guardian News and Media. Available at: https://www. theguardian.com/film/2015/jan/20/jane-fonda-hanoi-jane-photo-was-a-huge-mistake (Accessed: February 17, 2023).

Jeffrey, E., & Sportelli , N. (n.d.). *Adam Clayton Powell Jr., Class of 1930.* Colgate At 200 Years. Retrieved January 11, 2023, from https://200.colgate.edu/looking-back/people/adam-clayton-powell-jr-class-1930

Jim Crow to civil rights in Virginia (no date) *Virginia Museum of History & Culture.* Available at: https://virginiahistory. org/learn/jim-crow-civil-rights-virginia (Accessed: January 7, 2023).

Jim Crow Museum Available at: https://jimcrowmuseum. ferris.edu/what.htm (Accessed: August 26, 2023).

Karimi, F. (2018, May 25). https://lite.cnn.com/en/article/ h_332882ce032dc7cca274b635ce9a7b36. CNN. Retrieved June 11, 2019, from https://lite.cnn.com/en/article/ h_332882ce032dc7cca274b635ce9a7b36

Kendi, I. X. (2017, May 26). Colorism as racism: Garvey, Du Bois and the other color line. AAIHS. Retrieved January 12, 2023, from https://www.aaihs.org/colorism-as-racism-garvey-du-bois-and-the-other-color-line/

Kelley, R. D. G. (1990). *Hammer and Hoe*. University of North Carolina Press.

Loewy, D. and Guffey, M.E. (2013) Essentials of Business Communication. Mason, OH: SouthWestern/Cengage Learning.

Mack, K. & Palfrey, J. (2020). "Capitalizing Black and White: Grammatical Justice and Equity." RSS. Accessed January 8, 2023. https://www.macfound.org/press/perspectives/capitalizing-black-and-white-grammatical-justice-and-equity.

Maslow A. H. (1943). Theory of human motivation. *Psychological Review*, 50, 370–396.

Mays, J. and Jaffe, R. (2014) History Corrected—the scottsboro boys are officially innocent. Available at: https://www.rjaffelaw.com/documents/Jaffe_History_Corrected_March_2014.pdf (Accessed: January 14, 2023).

Military service quotes (no date) BrainyQuote. Xplore. Available at: https://www.brainyquote.com/topics/military-service-quotes (Accessed: January 16, 2023).

Military service. National Museum of American History. (2013, November 18). Retrieved January 12, 2023, from https://americanhistory.si.edu/changing-america-emancipation-proclamation-1863-and-march-washington-1963/1863/military-service

Milzarski, E. (2021) Radiomen in the Vietnam War faced a 5-Second Life Expectancy, We Are The Mighty. Available at: https://www.wearethemighty.com/mighty-history/radiomen-life-expectancy-vietnam-war/ (Accessed: January 16, 2023).

Mydans, S. (2000) Old wounds slow u.s.-vietnam reconciliation, The New York Times. The New York Times. Available at: https://www.nytimes.com/2000/04/29/world/old-wounds-slow-us-vietnam-reconciliation.html (Accessed: February 22, 2023).

Norwood, A.R. (no date) *Biography: Maggie Lena Walker*. Available at: https://www.womenshistory.org/education-resources/biographies/maggie-lena-walker (Accessed: January 7, 2023).

Norwood, Kimberly Jade. "'If You Is White, You's Alright ...'" Stories about Colorism in America." *Washington University Global Studies Law Review* 14, no. 4. (2015). Accessed December 30, 2019. https://openscholarship.wustl.edu/law_globalstudies/vol14/iss4/8/.

Office of the United States Trade Representative. "Vietnam." Accessed September 5, 2022. https://ustr.gov/countries-regions/southeast-asia-pacific/vietnam#:~:text=Goods%20exports%20totaled%20%249.9%20billion,services%20imports%20were%20%24461%20million.

Onion, Rebecca. (2022). "The Snake-Eaters and the Yards." *Slate*, November 27, 2013. Accessed September 5, 2022. https://slate.com/news-and-politics/2013/11/the-green-berets-and-the-montagnards-how-an-indigenous-tribe-won-the-admiration-of-green-berets-and-lost-everything.html.

Page, L. (2022, December 16). Before passing away, Carol Channing passed for White. BeaconBroadside: A Project of Beacon Press. Retrieved January 11, 2023, from https://www.beaconbroadside.com/broadside/2019/01/before-passing-away-carol-channing-passed-for-white.html

Powell, Adam Clayton Jr., *Adam by Adam: the Autobiography of Adam Clayton Powell Jr.*, New York, N.Y.: Kensington Publishers, 2002.

Roosevelt , F. (n.d.). FDR and the Four freedoms speech. FDR Presidential Library & Museum. Retrieved January 12, 2023, from https://www.fdrlibrary.org/four-freedoms

Rosenbaum, Ava. "Personal Space and American Individualism." *Brown Political Review*. October 31, 2018. Accessed September 24, 2022. https://brownpoliticalreview.org/2018/10/personal-space-american-individualism.

Rowse, A.F.P.B. (2003) White is beautiful in Vietnam, ThingsAsian. Things Asian Press. Available at: http://thingsasian.com/story/white-beautiful-vietnam (Accessed: February 5, 2023).

Schuessler, J. (2015) Use of 'African-American' dates to nation's early days, The New York Times.The New York Times. Available at: https://www.nytimes.com/2015/04/21/arts/use-of-african-american-dates-to-nations-early-days.html (Accessed: January 7, 2023).

Spagnoli, F. (2014) The Ethics of Human Rights (6): Human rights and Maslow's hierarchy of needs, The Ethics of Human Rights (6): Human Rights and Maslow's Hierarchy of Needs. *Available at: https://cosmologicallyinsignificant. wordpress.com/2008/08/27/human-rights-quote-86-human-rights-and-maslows-hierarchy-of-needs/ (Accessed: January 13, 2023).*

Solis, M. (2014) *Debate on human rights vs human needs.* Available at: https://www.adelaide.edu.au/news/news73183. html (Accessed: January 14, 2023).

Southerland, Dan. "An Update on the Montagnards of Vietnam's Central Highlands." *Radio Free Asia* (blog). October 23, 2018. Accessed September 5, 2022. https://www.rfa.org/english/commentaries/vietnam-montagnards-10232018155849.html.

Staff, L.M. (2017) Open the doors, Lynchburg. Available at: https://magazine.lynchburg.edu/article/open-the-doors/ (Accessed: February 1, 2023).

State of California North American Heritage Commission. "California Indian History." Accessed September 9, 2022. https://nahc.ca.gov/resources/california-indian-history/.

Thomas, William. "The Real Problem with Americans and Their Disrespect for Obama—according to a Canadian." *Quartz,* November 10, 2014. Accessed September 26, 2022. https://qz.com/293555/the-real-problem-with-americans-and-their-disrespect-for-obama-according-to-a-canadian/.

The Two-Way. "Comedian and Civil Rights Activist Dick Gregory Dies at 84." August 19, 2017. Accessed October 20, 2019. https://www.npr.org/sections/thetwo-way/2017/08/19/544769294/dick-gregory-comedian-and-civil-rights-activist-dies-at-84.

Tyson, Timothy. *The Blood of Emmett Till*. New York: Simon & Schuster, 2017.

United Press International. "New York's Biggest March—10 Years Late: Vietnam Veterans Get Their Parade at Last." *Los Angeles Times*, May 7, 1985. Accessed September 29, 2022. https://www.latimes.com/archives/la-xpm-1985-05-07-mn-11129-story.html.

U.S. Supreme Court of Appeals (2020) *Morgan v. Commonwealth (June 6, 1945)*, *Encyclopedia Virginia*. Available at: https://encyclopediavirginia.org/entries/morgan-v-commonwealth-june-6-1945/ (Accessed: January 7, 2023).

Vaughn, Skip. "Radio Operator Had Hazardous Duty in Vietnam." Redstone Rocket, October 14, 2015. Accessed September 10, 2022. https://www.theredstonerocket.com/news/article_4f80df0a-726f-11e5-b38e-ab069a8a1a91.html.

Verrengia, Joe, and Karle, Stuart. "Visions of America Clash at KKK Rally in Connecticut." *Columbia Spectator*, September 15, 1980. http://spectatorarchive.library.columbia.edu/cgi-bin/columbia?a=d&d=cs19800915-01.2.5&e=-------en-20--1--txt-IN-----.

Vietnam's blueprint for ethnic cleansing - europarl.europa.eu (no date). MONTAGNARD FOUNDATION, INC. Available at: https://www.europarl.europa.eu/meetdocs/2004_2009/documents/dv/droi_080825_ethnicleansingv/DROI_080825_EthnicleansingVen.pdf (Accessed: January 17, 2023).

Wallenstein, P. (2022, July 26). Desegregation in higher education. Encyclopedia Virginia. Retrieved January 30, 2023, from https://encyclopediavirginia.org/entries/desegregation-in-higher-education/#:~:text=Desegregation%20was%20 spurred%20on%20by,faculty%2C%20staff%2C%20 and%20administrators.

Whitman, Alden. "Ho Chi Minh Was Noted for Success in Blending Nationalism and Communism." *New York Times*, September 4, 1969. Accessed September 25, 2022. https:// archive.nytimes.com/www.nytimes.com/learning/general/ onthisday/bday/0519.html.

Williams, Fannie B. "Do We Need Another Name?" The Southern Workman XXXIII (January 1904): 31–36.

Wikipedia. "369th Infantry Regiment (United States)." Accessed September 25, 2022. https://en.wikipedia.org/ wiki/369th_Infantry_Regiment_(United_States).

Wikipedia. "Adam Clayton Powell Jr." Accessed November 23, 2019. https://en.wikipedia.org/wiki/Adam_Clayton_Powell_Jr.

Wikipedia. "DeWitt Clinton High School." Accessed September 25, 2022. https://en.wikipedia.org/wiki/DeWitt_Clinton_ High_School.

Winslow, Barbara. *Shirley Chisholm: Catalyst for Change.* Routledge, 2018.

Your rights under Title II - united states department of justice (no date) United States Department of Justice - Civil Rights Division. Available at: https://www.justice.gov/crt/ page/file/1251321/download (Accessed: January 14, 2023).

Zeleny, Jeff. "Reid Apologizes for Remarks on Obama's Skin Color and 'Dialect.'" The New York Times, January 9, 2010. Accessed December 15, 2019. https://www.nytimes. com/2010/01/10/us/politics/10reidweb.html.

Printed in the USA
CPSIA information can be obtained
at www.ICGtesting.com
JSHW021934021024
70959JS00004B/9